NATIONAL
PARK SERVICE
Camping Guide

Published by:

Roundabout Publications
PO Box 19235
Lenexa, KS 66285

800-455-2207

www.TravelBooksUSA.com

Please Note:

Every effort has been made to make this book as complete and as accurate as possible. However, there may be mistakes both typographical and in content. Therefore, this text should be used as a general guide to National Park Service campgrounds. Although we regret any inconvenience caused by inaccurate information, the author and Roundabout Publications shall have neither liability nor responsibility to any person or entity with respect to any loss or damage caused, or alleged to be caused, directly or indirectly by the information contained in this book.

National Park Service Camping Guide, copyright © 2004 by Roundabout Publications. Printed and bound in the United States of America. All rights reserved. No part of this book may be reproduced in any form or by any electronic or mechanical means including information storage and retrieval systems without permission in writing from the publisher, except by a reviewer, who may quote passages in a review. Published by Roundabout Publications, P.O. Box 19235, Lenexa, Kansas, 66285; phone: 800-455-2207; Internet: www.travelbooksusa.com

Library of Congress Control Number: 2003097496
ISBN: 1-885464-06-1

Publisher's Cataloging-in-Publication

Herow, William C.
        National Park Service camping guide / by William C. Herow. -- 2nd ed.
        p. cm.
        Includes index.
        LCCN: 2003097496
        ISBN: 1-885464-06-1

        1. Camp sites, facilities, etc.--United States--Directories. 2. National parks and reserves--United States--Directories. I. Title.

GV191.35.H47 2003   647.9473'09

Contents

Colorado   68

Florida   80

Georgia   87

Hawaii   89

Idaho   92

Indiana 95

Kentucky 97

Maine 100

Maryland 103

Massachusetts 109

Michigan 111

Minnesota 117

Mississippi 120

Missouri 122

Montana   125

Nevada   131

New Mexico   136

New York   142

North Carolina   144

North Dakota   151

Oklahoma   153

Oregon   155

Pennsylvania   157

South Carolina 159

South Dakota 162

Tennessee 165

Texas 171

Utah 183

Virgin Islands 195

Virginia   197

Washington   201

West Virginia   214

Wisconsin   217

Wyoming   221

Appendix A   228

Appendix B   230

Index   236

Introduction

The National Park Service

On August 25, 1916, President Woodrow Wilson signed the act creating the National Park Service, a new federal bureau in the Department of Interior. Its responsibility was to protect the 35 national parks and monuments then managed by the department and those yet to be established. Today the National Park Service is made up of 384 units covering more than 83 million acres.

About This Book

National Park Service Camping Guide brings together in one book all the National Park Service areas that offer some form of camping, whether it be in a developed campground or primitive camping in the backcountry. More than 100 areas are covered in this book.

National Park Service Areas

Each state begins with a list of the National Park Service areas in that state. Each is numbered and shown on a map. An *Activities Chart*, described below, summarizes the activities available in each area.

Activities Chart

The *Activities Chart* shows you at a glance the activities available in each National Park Service area. The icons across the top of the chart represent the type of activity and a "bullet" beneath indicates that the activity is available in the area. A sample chart is shown on the next page.

Activities Chart

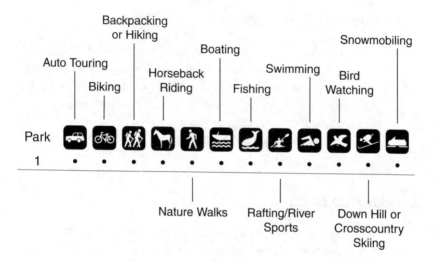

Contact Information

Contact information for each National Park Service area is listed directly beneath the area's name. You can use the address and phone number provided to obtain a detailed map and brochure for the areas you are interested in. Brochures are available free of charge.

Description

A brief description of each area follows the contact information. You'll find basic information about the area and whether an entrance fee is charged. The location of visitor centers is also mentioned. Visitor centers have free maps and brochures of the area and park rangers available to answer your questions.

Campground Listings

Campground listings provide specific information about each camping area. The location of each campground is generally given first followed by season of operation, number of sites, and cost per night. Other information about facilities or services available is then listed such as restrooms, showers, RV length limits, length of stay limits, etc.

A row of icons follows each campground listing that summarizes the facilities. This allows you to quickly scan the listings for specific facilities or services that you desire. A description of each icon is provided on the next page.

As mentioned above, RV length limits are given (if known) as part of each campground's description. Maximum lengths vary from park to park but the average is 27 feet. Some campgrounds can accommodate RVs up to 40 feet. It is a good idea to contact the park for specific information so you won't be surprised when you arrive.

Money Saving Programs

In Appendix A you will find money saving programs offered by the National Park Service. If you're a mature traveler interested in saving 50 percent on camping fees, be sure to look at the Golden Age Passport program.

Lodges in National Park Service Areas

In Appendix B you will find information about lodging establishments in National Park Service areas.

Campground Listing Icons

Cabins available for rent

Campsites suitable for RVs

Tent camping sites

Sites with electric hookups

Site with water hookups

Dump station available

Restrooms (pit, vault, flush)

Showers (hot or cold)

Drinking water available

Picnic table or picnic area

Swimming area

Hiking, backpacking, or nature trails

Bicycling trails

Off-road-vehicle trails

Equestrian trails

Boat launching ramp

Marina

Handicapped facilities

Alaska

1   Denali National Park & Preserve
2   Gates of the Arctic National Park & Preserve
3   Glacier Bay National Park & Preserve
4   Katmai National Park & Preserve
5   Kenai Fjords National Park
6   Klondike Gold Rush National Historical Park
7   Kobuk Valley National Park
8   Lake Clark National Park & Preserve
9   Wrangell-Saint Elias National Park & Preserve

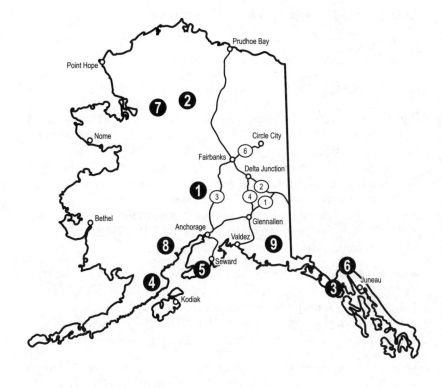

Activities Chart

Park	🚗	🚲	🥾	🐴	🚶	〰️	🦆	🛶	🏊	✈️	🎿	🛶
1		•	•		•					•	•	•
2		•			•				•	•		
3		•				•	•	•				
4		•		•	•	•	•	•		•	•	
5		•		•	•	•	•	•			•	
6	•	•	•	•	•	•	•	•		•	•	•
7		•			•	•					•	
8		•		•	•	•	•			•	•	•
9	•	•	•	•	•	•	•	•			•	•

Denali National Park & Preserve

PO Box 9
Denali Park, AK 99755
Phone: 907-683-2294
Fax: 907-683-9617

Denali National Park and Preserve is home to North America's highest mountain, 20,320-foot Mount McKinley. It was established as the Mount McKinley National Park in 1917. The original park was designated a wilderness area and incorporated into Denali National Park and Preserve in 1980. The park encompasses over 6 million acres. Private vehicle access into the park is restricted to the first 15 miles of Denali Park Road. To travel farther into the park, shuttle and tour bus services are available. Bicycles are permitted along the Park Road. Entrance fee is $5 per person or $10 per family (up to 8 people).

Information is available from two visitor centers. Denali National Park Visitor Center is one mile inside the park and is open 10:00 a.m. to 4:00 p.m., May through September. Eielson Visitor Center is at mile 66 of Denali Park Road and is open 9:00 a.m. to 7:00 p.m., June to mid-September; it can only be reached by shuttle bus.

There are six campgrounds within the park. Camping is limited to 14 days. Advance reservations are accepted for campsites at Riley Creek, Savage River, Teklanika River, and Wonder Lake campgrounds. Call 800-622-7275 or 907-272-7275. A one-time fee of $4 per campground site is charged. If you do not have advance reservations, plan to camp outside the park when you first arrive. There may be a two-night wait for park campsites.

- **Igloo Creek**: located near mile 34 of Denali Park Road, open mid-May to mid-September, 7 tent-only sites, $9 per night, access by shuttle bus only, no vehicles, no water, chemical toilets available.

- **Riley Creek**: located near park entrance, open all year, 100 sites, $18 per night, limited facilities September to May, flush toilets and pay phone available.

- **Sanctuary River**: located at mile 23 of Park Road, open mid-May to mid-September, 7 tent-only sites, $9 per night, accessible only by shuttle bus, no water, chemical toilets, no open fires - stoves only.

- **Savage River**: located at mile 13 of Park Road, open mid-May to mid-September, 33 sites, $18 per night, water and flush toilets available, campground hosts on site.

- **Teklanika River**: located at mile 29 of Park Road, open mid-May to mid-September, 53 sites, $16 per night, water and flush toilets available. RVers may drive to this campground but must stay a minimum of three nights. RVers who are driving to the campground should purchase a Teklanika Pass, a shuttle bus ticket good for the entire campground visit.

- **Wonder Lake**: located near mile 85 on Park Road, open mid-June to mid-September, 28 tent sites, $16 per night, access by shuttle bus only, water and flush toilets available, no open fires - stoves only.

Backcountry camping requires a permit, available for free at the visitor center. Permits are issued only one day in advance; reservations are not accepted. All areas require the use of bear resistant food containers, available free with your backcountry permit.

Gates of the Arctic National Park & Preserve

Bettles Ranger Station
PO Box 26030
Bettles, AK 99726
Phone: 907-692-5494
Fax: 907-692-5400

Gates of the Arctic National Park and Preserve encompasses nearly 8.5 million acres of pristine wilderness in Alaska's Brooks Range. The park is made up of several elements including the national park, national preserve, wilderness, six Wild Rivers, and two National Natural Landmarks. It is primarily inhabited by caribou, Dall sheep, wolves, barren-ground grizzlies and black bears. The park receives around 9,000 visitors annually in search of a unique wilderness experience. There are no entrance fees. All visitors are expected to participate in a free backcountry orientation program.

Access to the park is by air; scheduled air taxis from Fairbanks serve Anaktuvuk Pass, Bettles, and Coldfoot. Bush charters are available from Bettles and Coldfoot into the park. Travelers to Anaktuvuk Pass can hike into the park. Information is available from the Bettles Ranger Station, which is open 8:00 a.m. to 5:00 p.m. seven days a week from mid-June to Labor Day. The rest of the year it is open Monday through Friday from 8:00 a.m. to noon and 1:00 p.m. to 5:00 p.m. A visitor center is also located in Coldfoot that is open Memorial Day to Labor Day. There are no visitor centers or facilities of any kind within the park.

Visitors to this remote park must be well prepared and self sufficient. Wilderness skills are essential; you should spend some time studying topographic maps of the area. There are no roads or established trails within the park. Be prepared for emergencies and radical changes in the weather; it can snow at any time of the year. Always carry enough food for extra days because inclement weather can delay air service.

Glacier Bay National Park & Preserve

PO Box 140
Gustavus, AK 99826
Phone: 907-697-2230
Fax: 907-697-2654

Glacier Bay National Park and Preserve is in southeast Alaska. It contains 3,283,246 acres of snow-capped mountains, freshwater lakes, and coastal beaches. The park was first established as a National Monument in 1925 and a Park and Preserve in 1980. More than 400,000 visitors a year come to this beautiful park. There is no entrance fee.

Information is available from the Glacier Bay Visitor Center, which is located on the second level of the Glacier Bay Lodge in Bartlett Cove. The center is open mid-May to mid-September. Exhibits illustrate the park's natural and cultural history. Park rangers offer evening programs and films in the auditorium.

There is one campground in the park. All campers are required to attend a free camper orientation, which is given on demand at the visitor information station. Visitors can obtain a backcountry camping permit and check out a bear-resistant food canister at the information center.

- **Bartlett Cove**: located about one-quarter mile by trail from the main dock, open May through September, 35 campsites, no fee is charged but a permit is required, warming shelter, outhouses, bear-resistant food storage, 14 day maximum stay.

Katmai National Park & Preserve

PO Box 7
King Salmon, AK 99613
Phone: 907-271-3751 or 907-246-3305
Fax: 907-246-2116

Katmai National Park and Preserve is known for volcanoes, brown bears, fish, and rugged wilderness. It's also the site of the Brooks River National Historic Landmark, which contains the highest concentration of prehistoric human dwellings in North America. The 4.1 million acre park is accessible only by boat or plane, yet more than 50,000 visitors come to this park each year. Katmai was designated a National Monument in 1918 and a National Park in 1980. The park's headquarters is in King Salmon, about 290 air miles southwest of Anchorage. Several commercial airlines provide daily flights into King Salmon.

A common destination for most visitors is Brooks Camp, about 30 air miles from King Salmon. There is a user fee of $10 per person, per day. All visitors to Brooks Camp are required to attend the Brooks Camp School of Bear Etiquette offered at the visitor center. Peak season for viewing brown bears is late June through July and in September.

There is one primitive campground in the park. Backcountry camping is also permitted.

- **Brooks Camp**: open June to mid-September, 60 sites, $8 per person per night (in addition to daily user fee), advance reservations and fee payment required (800-365-2267), drinking water, pit toilets, fire pits, picnic tables, bear-resistant food storage.

Kenai Fjords National Park

PO Box 1727
Seward, AK 99664
Phone: 907-224-2132 or 907-224-3175
Fax: 907-224-2144

Kenai Fjords National Park lies south of Seward in south-central Alaska. It encompasses nearly 670,000 acres of rugged, pristine land. The fjords are long, steep-sided, glacier-carved valleys now filled with ocean water. Beyond the coastline, mountains rise dramatically. The park contains much of the 300-square mile Harding Icefield, some 35 miles long and 20 miles wide. Exit Glacier spills off the icefield and is popular with visitors as it can be reached by road. There is an entrance fee of $5 and additional user fees at Exit Glacier.

A visitor center in Seward offers exhibits, maps, publications, and other information. It is open Monday through Friday year-round, and Saturdays and Sundays from Memorial Day through Labor Day. Information is also available from the ranger station at Exit Glacier.

There is a campground with 12 walk-in sites at Exit Glacier. Three backcountry cabins, located in the fjords of Holgate Arm, Aialik Bay, and North Arm, are available in summer. A public use cabin is available in winter at Exit Glacier. Cabin stays are limited to three days. Visitors must obtain reservations and permits in advance.

Klondike Gold Rush National Historical Park

PO Box 517
Skagway, AK 99840
Phone: 907-983-9224 or 907-983-2921
Fax: 907-983-9249

Klondike Gold Rush National Historical Park is in southeast Alaska in Skagway, which is about 80 miles by air north of Juneau. It celebrates the Klondike Gold Rush of 1897-98 through 15 restored buildings within the Skagway Historic District. The park also preserves a portion of the Chilkoot and White Pass Trails and the Dyea Townsite at the foot of Chilkoot Trail. A permit is required to hike the U.S. and Canadian portions of the Chilkoot Trail. The U.S. permit is free.

Information is available from the visitor center located inside the restored railway depot building at Broadway and Second Avenue. The center is open year-round.

There is only one campground available to visitors.

- **Dyea**: located ten miles from Skagway near the old townsite of Dyea, open mid-May through September, 22 rustic sites, $5 per night, fire rings, picnic tables, pit toilets, no hookups, visitors are advised to bring drinking water and firewood.

Kobuk Valley National Park

PO Box 1029
Kotzebue, AK 99752
Phone: 907-442-3890 or 907-442-3760
Fax: 907-442-8316

Kobuk Valley National Park preserves approximately 1.7 million acres of land in northern Alaska. Contained within the park is the Great Kobuk Sand Dunes, a 25-square mile area of shifting sand dunes where summer temperatures can exceed 90 degrees. Another attraction is the slow-moving and gentle Kobuk River, which is popular for fishing, canoeing, or kayaking. Access to the park is by air. Commercial airlines provide service from Anchorage or Fairbanks to Nome and Kotzebue. Visitors may then fly to the parklands and nearby villages.

A Public Lands Information Center is located in Kotzebue. Throughout the year educational and interpretive programs are offered. The center is open daily from 8:00 a.m. to 6:00 p.m. during summer. Winter hours vary.

Visitors to this remote park must be well prepared and self sufficient. Wilderness skills are essential; you should spend some time studying topographic maps of the area. There are no roads or established trails within the park and no developed camping areas. Tundra and river bars are often used as campsites. Kobuk Valley National Park contains many unmarked parcels of private land, check with the information center for more information.

Lake Clark National Park & Preserve

Field Headquarters
1 Park Place
Port Alsworth, AK 99653
Phone: 907-271-3751 or 907-781-2218
Fax: 907-781-2119

Lake Clark National Park and Preserve is in south-central Alaska. It covers more than 4 million acres of land, stretching from the shores of Cook Inlet, across the Chigmit Mountains, to the tundra covered hills of the western interior. Annually, around 6,000 visitors come to this park. Numerous lakes and rivers offer excellent fishing and wildlife viewing opportunities. There is no road access to the park; a one to two-hour flight from Anchorage, Kenai or Homer provides access to most points within the park.

A visitor center is in Port Alsworth on the shores of Lake Clark. It is open 8:00 a.m. to 5:00 p.m. from May through October. The rest of the year it is open on request. Exhibits and information about the area are available.

There are no roads within the park. A 2½-mile trail to Tanalian Falls and Kontrashibuna Lake is accessible from the town of Port Alsworth. There are no developed camping areas within the park, however, camping is permitted throughout the park. No permit is required. Visitors that plan on backcountry camping should be well prepared and self sufficient. Wilderness skills are essential.

Wrangell-Saint Elias National Park & Preserve

PO Box 439
Copper Center, AK 99573
Phone: 907-822-5234 or 907-822-5238
Fax: 907-822-7216

This huge 13.2 million acre park is located in
southeast Alaska. Here, the Chugach, Wrangell, and Saint Elias
mountain ranges converge. The park contains America's largest
collection of glaciers and mountains above 16,000 feet. Mount Saint
Elias, at 18,008 feet, is the second highest peak in the United States.
Around 30,000 visitors come to the park annually in search of a unique
wilderness experience. There is no entrance fee.

Two unpaved roads enter the park: McCarthy Road and Nabesna Road.
Both roads lead to historic mining towns. Near the park entrance on
McCarthy Road is the Chitina Ranger Station where information is
available. It is open during the summer. On Nabesna Road near the
park's entrance is the Slana Ranger Station; it is also open during
summer. The park's headquarters is located at mile 106.8 on Richardson
Highway. It remains open year-round.

There are no developed campgrounds within the park. Backcountry
camping is permitted nearly anywhere within the park's boundary.
Wilderness skills are essential. Visitors planning on camping in the
backcountry should complete a "Backcountry Trip Itinerary," available
at the visitor center and both ranger stations. Camping is also available
at a number of roadside pullouts along Nabesna Road, some with picnic
tables and pit toilets. Developed campgrounds may be found outside
the park along Richardson Highway.

There are currently 14 cabins available for public use on a first-come,
first-served basis. A reservation system is not in place at present. Users
should not expect amenities or furnishings of any kind. The cabins do
contain a wood-burning stove and bunks. Users should replenish any
firewood stored in the cabins for the next user.

Arizona

1 Canyon De Chelly National Monument
2 Chiricahua National Monument
3 Glen Canyon National Recreation Area, *see Utah*
4 Grand Canyon National Park
5 Lake Mead National Recreation Area, *see Nevada*
6 Navajo National Monument
7 Organ Pipe Cactus National Monument
8 Petrified Forest National Park
9 Saguaro National Park
10 Sunset Crater Volcano National Monument

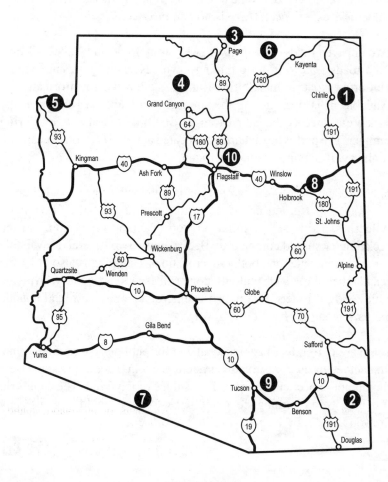

Activities Chart

Park												
1	•		•	•								
2	•		•						•			
4	•	•	•	•	•		•	•		•	•	
6		•		•								
7	•	•	•	•	•				•			
8	•	•	•	•	•				•			
9	•	•	•		•				•			
10		•										

Canyon De Chelly National Monument

PO Box 588
Chinle, AZ 86503
Phone: 928-674-5500
Fax: 928-674-5507

Canyon de Chelly National Monument is in the Navajo Reservation three miles east of Chinle and 200 miles northeast of Flagstaff. The nearly 84,000-acre park contains ruins of Indian villages constructed between 350 and 1300 A.D. The park remains open all year. No entrance fee is charged. To drive on the canyon bottom requires a four-wheel drive vehicle, a Park Service permit, and an authorized Navajo guide. The fee is $15 per hour for one vehicle. Hiking within the canyon requires a permit and an authorized Navajo guide, except along the 2.5-mile White House Ruins Trail.

Information is available from the Canyon de Chelly Visitor Center, located three miles east of US 191 in Chinle. It is open year-round and has exhibits featuring the cultural history of the area.

There is only one campground available to visitors. All campsites are available on a first-come, first-served basis; reservations are not accepted. Backcountry camping is permitted with an authorized guide.

- **Cottonwood**: near visitor center, 95 sites, no fee, five day maximum stay, 35-foot RV length limit, drinking water, flush toilets, dump station, limited facilities in winter.

Chiricahua National Monument

13063 E Bonita Canyon Rd
Willcox, AZ 85643
Phone: 520-824-3560
Fax: 520-824-3421

Chiricahua National Monument is in southeast Arizona about 36 miles
southeast of Willcox and 100 miles east of Tucson. The park preserves
12,000 acres of the Chiricahua Mountains and unusual rock formations.
An entrance fee of $5 per person is charged.

Information is available from the Chiricahua Visitor Center located
two miles from the monument entrance. It is open all year between
8:00 a.m. and 5:00 p.m. and has audiovisual programs, exhibits, and
books for sale.

There is only one campground within the monument. Campsites are
available on a first-come, first-served basis; reservations not accepted.
Backcountry camping is not permitted. There is no food service,
gasoline, or lodging within the monument. Supplies can be obtained
from nearby communities.

- **Bonita Canyon**: open all year, 25 sites, no hookups, $12 per night, 26-
  foot RV length limit, restrooms, water, picnic tables, 14 day stay limit.

Grand Canyon National Park

PO Box 129
Grand Canyon, AZ 86023
Phone: 928-638-7888
Fax: 928-638-7797

Grand Canyon National Park is located in northern Arizona. It encompasses 277 miles of the Colorado River and 1.2 million acres of land. Nearly five million people visit the park annually; visitation is highest in spring, summer, and fall. Reservations for camping and lodging are essential during this time. At the entrance station (either North or South Rim) you will receive an informative paper detailing parking areas, ranger programs, and visitor facilities. An entrance fee of $10 for individuals or $20 for vehicles is charged.

Visitor information is available from three locations in the park. The first is Canyon View Information Plaza, located at Mather Point. It is open all year between 8:00 a.m. and 5:00 p.m. The Desert View Information Center is located at the park's east entrance on the South Rim. It is open all year between 9:00 a.m. and 5:00 p.m. The North Rim Visitor Center is adjacent to the parking lot on Bright Angel Peninsula and is open mid-May to mid-October between 8:00 a.m. and 6:00 p.m.

There are three developed campgrounds operated by the National Park Service and one operated by a concessionaire. Backcountry camping is available and requires a permit. There is a $10 fee for the permit plus an additional fee of $5 per night, per person.

- **Desert View**: located 25 miles east of Grand Canyon Village on the South Rim, open mid-April through mid-October, available on a first-come, first-served basis (no reservations accepted), 50 RV and tent sites, seven day maximum stay, $12 per night, no hookups, 40-foot RV length limit.

- **Mather**: located in Grand Canyon Village on the South Rim, open all year, 318 RV and tent sites, no hookups, seven day maximum stay, reservations strongly recommended mid-March through October (call 1-800-365-2267), reservations may be made up to five months in advance, $15 per night April through November, $10 per night December through March (reservations not needed, first-come, first-served).

- **Trailer Village**: concessionaire-operated campground adjacent to Mather Campground, open all year, 78 RV sites, $25 per night, reservations recommended (888-297-2757), full hookups, 50-foot RV length limit, seven day maximum stay, showers and laundry facilities nearby.

- **North Rim**: located off AZ 67 near North Rim, open mid-May to mid-October, 83 RV and tent sites, $15 per night, no hookups, dump station available, seven day maximum stay, reservations accepted (1-800-365-2267), showers and laundry facilities nearby.

Navajo National Monument

HC 71 Box 3
Tonalea, AZ 86044
Phone: 928-672-2700
Fax: 928-672-2703

Navajo National Monument is in northeast Arizona about 140 miles north of Flagstaff. It preserves three cliff dwellings of the Anasazi. The monument is high on the Shonto Plateau, overlooking the Tsegi Canyon system in the Navajo Nation. Rangers guide visitors on tours of the Keet Seel and Betatakin cliff dwellings. There is no entrance fee.

Information is available from the visitor center located nine miles north of Black Mesa Junction with US 160 on AZ 564. It is open all year except Thanksgiving Day, Christmas, and New Year's Day. Exhibits feature various artifacts from Anasazi and Navajo culture. A craft shop is also within the visitor center building.

One small campground is available to visitors. Campsites are available on a first-come, first-served basis; no reservations accepted. No open-flame fires are allowed; campers must use campstoves for cooking. In the summer, overflow space is available at an older, more primitive campground one mile north of the main campground.

- **Sunset View**: located near visitor center, open all year, 31 sites, restrooms, water, picnic tables, 28-foot RV length limit, seven day maximum stay, one handicapped-accessible campsite, no camping fee, no hookups.

Organ Pipe Cactus National Monument

10 Organ Pipe Dr
Ajo, AZ 85321
Phone: 520-387-6849
Fax: 520-387-7144

Organ Pipe Cactus National Monument is in southern Arizona about 140 miles south of Phoenix and 22 miles south of Why. It protects over 330,000 acres of Sonoran Desert wildlife and landscape. The monument exhibits an extraordinary collection of plants, including the organ pipe cactus, a large cactus rarely found in the United States. An entrance fee of $5 per vehicle is charged.

Information is available from the Twin Peaks Visitor Center, located on AZ 85 about 35 miles south of Ajo. The center is open year-round between 8:00 a.m. and 5:00 p.m. except on Christmas Day. Ranger conducted activities are generally available January through March. The center features a museum with photographic exhibit and dioramas on the Sonoran Desert.

There are two campgrounds within the monument. Campsites in both are available on a first-come, first-served basis. Generators are allowed to run only between noon and 4:00 p.m. Quiet hours are between 10:00 p.m. and 6:00 a.m.

- **Alamo**: open all year, primitive campground, four sites, $6 per night, no water, pit toilets, motorhomes and vehicles pulling trailers not allowed.

- **Twin Peak**: located along AZ 85, open all year, 208 RV/tent sites, $10 per night, 35-foot RV length limit, 14 day maximum stay mid-January through April, 30 day maximum stay rest of year, water, restrooms, picnic tables, grills, dump station.

Petrified Forest National Park

PO Box 2217
Petrified Forest National Park, AZ 86028
Phone: 928-524-6228
Fax: 928-524-3567

Petrified Forest National Park is in northeast Arizona and features one of the world's largest and most colorful concentrations of petrified wood. Among the park's 93,533 acres are the multi-hued badlands of the Chinle Formation known as the Painted Desert, historic structures, archeological sites, and displays of 225 million-year-old fossils. An entrance fee of $10 is charged and is good for seven days.

Information is available from one of two visitor centers. The first is located near the park's northern entrance off I-40 Exit 311. It is open all year between 8:00 a.m. and 5:00 p.m. and has general park information and a 20-minute video shown every half-hour. The second is located inside the Rainbow Forest Museum, near the park's southern entrance off US 180. It remains open year-round between 8:00 a.m. and 5:00 p.m. and has exhibits of early reptiles, dinosaurs, and petrified wood.

There are no developed campgrounds within the park, but nearby communities offer full service accommodations. Overnight backpacking is available in the Painted Desert Wilderness. A free permit is required and can be obtained at either the Painted Desert Visitor Center or Rainbow Forest Museum.

Saguaro National Park

3693 S Old Spanish Trail
Tucson, AZ 85730
Phone: 520-733-5153 or 520-733-5100
Fax: 520-733-5183

Saguaro National Park is in southern Arizona. It is divided into two districts: Saguaro East, or the Rincon Mountain District and Saguaro West, or the Tucson Mountain District. The park encompasses a total of 91,443 acres. A $6 fee is charged for entrance into Saguaro East. There is no charge for entrance into Saguaro West. Both districts have miles of trails for hiking and scenic loop drives.

Information is available from visitor centers in each district. Both are open all year between 8:30 a.m. and 5:00 p.m. daily except Christmas. Both offer slide shows, museums, cactus gardens, and a sales outlet.

There is no developed campground in either district. Backcountry camping is permitted in the Saguaro Wilderness Area located in Saguaro East. Reservations and a permit ($6 fee) is required and can be obtained at the visitor center. Permits are not available after noon on the day of departure. Campgrounds for RVs can be found in the surrounding area.

Sunset Crater Volcano National Monument

Flagstaff Area National Monuments - SUCR
6400 N Hwy 89
Flagstaff, AZ 86004
Phone: 928-526-0502
Fax: 928-526-4259

Sunset Crater Volcano National Monument is in north-central Arizona about 20 miles north of Flagstaff. The main attraction is a large cinder cone rising 1,000 feet above the surrounding landscape. Visitors will also find pueblos and cliff dwellings. The monument is open year-round and charges an entrance fee of $5 per person.

Information is available from the visitor center located two miles east of US 89 on Sunset Crater Wupatki Loop Road. The visitor center is open year-round. In March, April, May, September, and October the center is open between 8:00 a.m. and 5:00 p.m. June through August, the center is open 8:00 a.m. to 6:00 p.m. In January, February, and December the hours are 9:00 a.m. to 5:00 p.m. Special programs are generally offered during summer months.

There is one campground available to visitors. Bonito Campground is just outside the monument's boundary and is managed by the National Forest Service. For campground information contact the U.S. Forest Service at 928-526-0866.

- **Bonito**: located near the visitor center, open May to mid-October, 44 RV and tent sites, $12 per night during peak season (mid-May to mid-September), $8 per night off season, 42-foot RV length limit, drinking water, flush toilets, no hookups, 14 day maximum stay.

Arkansas

1   Buffalo National River
2   Hot Springs National Park

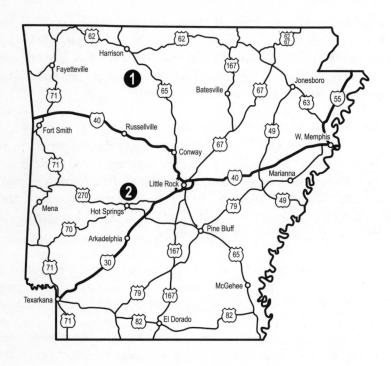

Activities Chart

Buffalo National River

402 N Walnut, Suite 136
Harrison, AR 72601
Phone: 870-741-5443 or 870-439-2502
Fax: 870-741-7286

Buffalo National River preserves 135 miles of the 150-mile long river running across northern Arkansas. It begins as a trickle in the Boston Mountains 15 miles above the park boundary and runs east through the Ozarks into the White River. Massive limestone bluffs contain the free-flowing river. There is no entrance fee.

Information is available from the Tyler Bend Visitor Center, which is located 11 miles north of Marshall on US 65. The center is open Thursday through Monday between 8:00 a.m. and 5:00 p.m. in summer and 8:30 a.m. to 4:30 p.m. the rest of the year. It is closed on Thanksgiving Day, Christmas Day, and New Year's Day. Information is also available from the Buffalo Point Campground Information Station, Buffalo Point Ranger Station, and Pruitt Ranger Station.

There are 13 campgrounds within Buffalo National River. Only one, Lost Valley, is not located along the river. Campsites in all campgrounds are available on a first-come, first-served basis.

- **Buffalo Point**: located 17 miles southeast of Yellville on AR 268, open all year, 83 RV sites with water and electric hookups ($17 per night), 20 walk in tent sites ($10 per night), three sites accessible to the handicapped, 31-foot RV length limit, 14 day maximum stay, picnic tables, fire grates, drinking water, showers, flush toilets, pay phone, dump station, facilities limited in winter.

- **Carver**: located south of Hasty off AR 123, open all year, eight sites, $10 per night April through October, picnic tables, vault toilets.

- **Erbie**: located eight miles west of Dogpatch via local road, open all year, primitive campground with 14 drive-in sites and 16 walk-in sites, picnic tables, fire grates, drinking water, flush and vault toilets, pay phone, $10

per night April through October.

- **Hasty**: located three miles west of Hasty along Low Water Bridge Road, open all year, primitive campground with two sites, picnic tables, vault toilets, no camping fee.

- **Kyles Landing**: located about seven miles west of Jasper off AR 74 via Kyles Landing Road, open all year, 33 sites, $10 per night April through October, picnic tables, fire grates, drinking water, flush toilets.

- **Lost Valley**: located two miles south of Ponca off AR 43, open all year, 15 sites, two sites accessible to the handicapped, $10 per night April through October, picnic tables, fire grates, drinking water, flush toilets.

- **Maumee South**: located 12 miles northwest of Harriet off AR 27 via CR 52, open all year, primitive campground with open camping, vault toilets, no camping fee.

- **Mount Hersey**: located ten miles south of Western Grove off US 65 via Mount Hersey Road, open all year, primitive campground with open camping, fire grates, vault toilets, no camping fee.

- **Ozark**: located six miles north of Jasper off AR 7, open all year, 35 sites, $10 per night April through October, picnic tables, fire grates, drinking water, flush toilets, pay phone.

- **Rush**: located six miles east of Caney off AR 14 via CR 26, open all year, 12 sites, $10 per night April through October, drinking water, fire grates, vault toilets, no camping fee.

- **Steel Creek**: located four miles northeast of Ponca off AR 74 via Steel Creek Road, open all year, 26 sites, $10 per night April through October, picnic tables, fire grates, drinking water, vault toilets, pay phone. Additional horse campground with 14 sites available.

- **Tyler Bend**: located 12 miles northwest of Marshall off US 65 via CR 241 and CR 231, open all year, 28 drive-in sites and ten walk-in sites, $10 per night April through October, picnic tables, fire grates, drinking water, showers, flush toilets, dump station, pay phone, no hookups, 28-foot RV length limit, 14 day maximum stay.

- **Woolum**: located seven miles southwest of Saint Joe off US 65 via AR 374 and CR 14, open all year, primitive campground with open camping, fire grates, vault toilets, no camping fee, horse campsites available.

Hot Springs National Park

PO Box 1860
Hot Springs, AR 71902
Phone: 501-624-2701
Fax: 501-624-3458

Hot Springs National Park is in central Arkansas about 50 miles southwest of Little Rock. It was first established as Hot Springs Reservation on April 20, 1832 to protect hot springs flowing from the southwestern slope of Hot Springs Mountain. It became Hot Springs National Park by a Congressional name change on March 4, 1921. The park protects eight historic bathhouses with the former luxurious Fordyce Bathhouse housing the visitor center. The park covers about 5,500 acres and attracts 3.2 million visitors annually.

Information is available from the visitor center located in the former Fordyce Bathhouse on Bathhouse Row in downtown Hot Springs. Bathhouse Row is on AR 7 (Central Avenue) between Reserve and Fountain Streets. The visitor center is open 9:00 a.m. to 5:00 p.m. year-round except New Year's Day, Thanksgiving Day, and Christmas Day. In summer the visitor center closes at 6:00 p.m.

There is one campground in the park. It is located on the eastern edge of Hot Springs, just off US 70. National Forest Service, Corps of Engineers, and state-managed campgrounds are also nearby.

- **Gulpha Gorge**: open year-round, 43 RV and tent sites, sites available on a first-come, first-served basis (no reservations accepted), drinking water, picnic tables, restrooms, dump station, pay phone, no hookups, $10 per night, 14 day maximum stay.

California

1 Channel Islands National Park
2 Death Valley National Park
3 Devil's Postpile National Monument
4 Golden Gate National Recreation Area
5 Joshua Tree National Park
6 Lassen Volcanic National Park
7 Lava Beds National Monument

8 Mojave National Preserve
9 Point Reyes National Seashore
10 Redwood National and State Parks
11 Santa Monica Mountains National Recreation Area
12 Sequoia & Kings Canyon National Parks
13 Whiskeytown National Recreation Area
14 Yosemite National Park

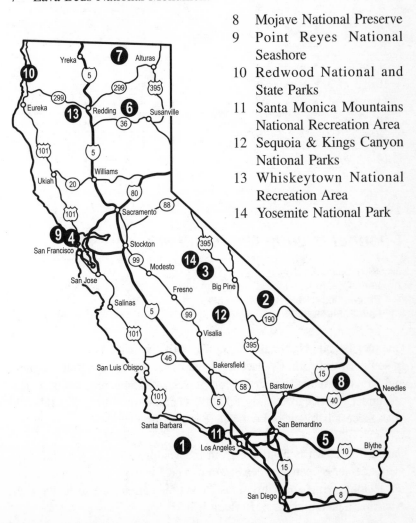

Activities Chart

Park	🚗	🚲	🥾	🐎	🧗	〰	🦆	🛶	🏊	🎿	🏄	⛺
1		•		•	•	•	•	•	•	•		
2	•	•	•	•	•					•	•	
3			•	•	•		•				•	•
4	•	•	•	•	•	•	•	•	•	•		
5	•	•	•	•	•				•			
6	•		•			•	•	•	•	•	•	•
7	•	•	•	•							•	
8	•	•	•	•	•				•			
9			•	•	•			•		•		
10	•	•	•	•	•	•	•	•	•	•		
11		•	•	•	•	•	•		•	•		
12	•		•	•	•		•			•	•	
13		•	•	•	•	•	•	•	•	•		
14	•	•	•	•	•	•	•	•	•	•	•	

Channel Islands National Park

1901 Spinnaker Dr
Ventura, CA 93001
Phone: 805-658-5730 or 805-658-5711
Fax: 805-658-5799

Channel Islands National Park consists of five islands
in southern California: Anacapa, Santa Cruz, Santa Rosa, San Miguel,
and Santa Barbara. The park encompasses 249,354 acres, half of which
are under the ocean. Nearly 650,000 visitors come to this park each
year. Access is by air or boat. There is no entrance fee.

Park information is available from the visitor center in Ventura. The
visitor center is open between 8:30 a.m. and 5:00 p.m. year-round except
on Thanksgiving and Christmas. A visitor center is also located on
Anacapa Island and Santa Barbara Island.

Camping is available on all five islands. A fee of $7.35 per night is charged for camping in all campgrounds. Advance reservations can be made for any of the campgrounds by calling 1-800-365-2267. A reservation fee of $2.65 per night is charged. Campers must be prepared for primitive camping and bring their own supplies, including a camp stove, fuel, and water. Supplies and equipment are not available on the islands. Be prepared to carry your camping gear from the landing areas to the campgrounds. All campers must pack out their own trash.

- **Anacapa Island**: open all year, seven campsites with a campground capacity of 30 people, pit toilets, picnic tables. The campground is one-half mile from the dock landing, up 154 steps.

- **San Miguel Island**: open all year, nine campsites with a total capacity of 30 people, pit toilets, picnic tables. The campground is a one-mile hike uphill from the beach landing.

- **Santa Barbara Island**: open all year, eight campsites with a total capacity of 30 people, pit toilets, picnic tables. The campground is one-half mile uphill from the dock landing.

- **Santa Cruz Island**: open all year, 40 sites that can accommodate four to six people per site, pit toilets, picnic tables. Potable water is provided at two taps in the lower campground. Campsites are spread out along the valley floor one-half to one mile up the flats from the beach landing.

- **Santa Rosa Island**: open year-round, 15 campsites with a total capacity of 50 people, pit toilets, picnic tables, running water (most people bring drinking water), shower facilities. Camping on the beach is permitted on a seasonal basis for experienced kayakers and boaters.

Death Valley National Park

PO Box 579
Death Valley, CA 92328
Phone: 760-786-3200
Fax: 760-786-3283

Death Valley National Park in southern California has more than 3.3 million acres of spectacular desert scenery. It contains the lowest point in the western hemisphere; Badwater is 282 feet below sea level. More than one million visitors come to this park each year. An entrance fee of $5 is charged for individuals or $10 for vehicles.

Information is available from the Beatty Information Center in Beatty, Nevada. Beatty is one of the eastern portals to Death Valley National Park. Stovepipe Wells Ranger Station is located in the center of Death Valley. General information and backcountry permits are available here.

There are nine designated camping areas in Death Valley National Park. Backcountry camping is permitted but your campsite must be two miles away from any developed area, paved road, or day-use area. Free permits may be obtained at the visitor center or ranger station.

- **Emigrant**: located along CA 190 about 18 miles east of Panamint Springs, open all year, ten tent-only sites, water, picnic tables, flush toilets, no fires allowed, no camping fee.

- **Furnace Creek**: located along CA 190 about 53 miles east of Panamint Springs, open all year, reservations accepted (1-800-365-2267), 136 RV and tent sites, drinking water, tables, fireplaces, flush toilets, dump station, no hookups, $16 per night during winter and $10 per night during summer, 14 day maximum stay, 35-foot RV length limit.

- **Mahogany Flat**: located in the Panamint Mountains off Emigrant Canyon Road, open March through November, accessible to high-clearance vehicles only, ten campsites, tables, fireplaces, pit toilets, no camping fee,

30 day maximum stay.

- **Mesquite Spring**: located five miles south of Scotty's Castle on Grapevine Road, open all year, 30 sites, water, tables, fireplaces, flush toilets, dump station, $10 per night, 30 day maximum stay, 35-foot RV length limit.

- **Stovepipe Wells**: located in Stovepipe Wells Village along CA 190, open mid-October to mid-April, 190 sites, some tables, some fireplaces, flush toilets, dump station, water, $10 per night, 30 day maximum stay, 35-foot RV length limit.

- **Sunset**: in Furnace Creek off CA 190, open mid-October to mid-April, 1000 RV/tent sites, water, flush toilets, dump station, no fires allowed, $10 per night, 30 day maximum stay, 40-foot RV length limit.

- **Texas Spring**: located one-half mile east of Furnace Creek off CA 190, open mid-October to mid-April, 92 sites, water, tables, fireplaces, flush toilets, dump station, $12 per night, 30 day maximum stay, 35-foot RV length limit. From mid-March to mid-April, the campground is designated primarily for tent camping with a limited number of RV sites.

- **Thorndike**: in the Panamint Mountains off Emigrant Canyon Road, open March through November, accessible to high-clearance vehicles only, six sites, tables, fireplaces, pit toilets, no camping fee, 30 day maximum stay.

- **Wildrose**: located in the Panamint Mountains off Emigrant Canyon Road, open all year, 23 sites, no camping fee, tables, fireplaces, pit toilets, 30 day maximum stay. Drinking water is available in spring, summer, and fall.

Devil's Postpile National Monument

PO Box 3999
Mammoth Lakes, CA 93546
Phone: 760-934-2289

Devil's Postpile National Monument is in central
California about 50 miles northwest of Bishop. It encompasses 800
acres and features the unusual geologic formation known as "the
Postpile." Nearly 75 percent of the monument is preserved as part of
the Ansel Adams Wilderness. The John Muir and Pacific Crest Trails
can be accessed within the monument. Devil's Postpile is open only in
summer. Except for vehicles with camping permits, private vehicles
are not allowed into the monument; a shuttle bus takes day-use visitors
into the monument. An entrance fee of $7 per person is charged. Please
note: The U.S. Forest Service, which manages land surrounding the
national monument, established this fee in 2002. The fee is required to
visit Devil's Postpile National Monument and is not covered by the
National Parks Pass.

Information is available from the Devil's Postpile Ranger Station located
just inside the monument's only entrance. The station is open in July
and August between 7:00 a.m. and 6:00 p.m.

There is only one National Park Service campground within the
monument. A camping permit is required. The U.S. Forest Service
manages five campgrounds a short distance from the monument.
Campsites are available on a first-come, first-served basis.

- **Devil's Postpile**: located near the ranger station, open July to mid-October
  depending on weather, 21 sites, $14 per night, flush toilets, 14 day maximum
  stay. Bear-resistant food boxes are provided.

Golden Gate National Recreation Area

Fort Mason, Building 201
San Francisco, CA 94123
Phone: 415-561-4700
Fax: 415-561-4750

Golden Gate National Recreation Area is in northern California northwest of San Francisco. It covers about 74,000 acres of land and water, making it the largest urban national park in the world. Approximately 28 miles of coastline lie within its boundaries. No entrance fee charged.

Information is available from the recreation area's headquarters at Fort Mason, which is at the cross streets of Bay and Franklin in San Francisco. The information center is open all year, Monday through Friday, between 10:00 a.m. and 4:30 p.m. Information about all the National Park Service areas in the region can be obtained here. Information can also be obtained from the Alcatraz Island Visitor Center, Cliff House Visitor Center, Marin Headlands Visitor Center, Muir Woods Visitor Center, and William Penn Mott Jr. Visitor Center on the Presidio of San Francisco.

Golden Gate National Recreation Area offers two hike-in and two walk-in campgrounds. The park does not have accommodations for recreational vehicles. Numerous other campgrounds, both private and public, can be found in the area.

- **Bicentennial**: walk-in campground located near Battery Wallace Picnic Area, open all year, three sites, no fee, portable toilets available, water at the visitor center one mile away, camp stoves permitted, no ground fires, three day maximum stay per year.

- **Hawkcamp**: hike-in campground open year-round, three sites, no camping fee, chemical toilets, picnic tables, no water, campstoves permitted, no ground fires, three day maximum stay per year.

- **Haypress**: hike-in campground located in the Tennessee Valley in the north end of Marin Highlands, open all year, five sites, no fee, portable restrooms, picnic tables, camp stoves permitted, no ground fires, no water, maximum three day stay per year.

- **Kirby Cove**: walk-in campground located west of the Golden Gate Bridge, open April through October, four sites, $25 per night, pit toilets, picnic tables, no water, reservations required (800-365-2267), three day maximum stay per year.

Joshua Tree National Park

74485 National Park Dr
Twentynine Palms, CA 92277
Phone: 760-367-5500
Fax: 760-367-6392

Joshua Tree National Park is in southern California. It covers more than one million acres and receives 1.3 million visitors annually. The Colorado Desert makes up the eastern part of the park. It features natural gardens of creosote bush, ocotillo, and cholla cactus. The western part of the park is higher, moister, and slightly cooler. It is here, in the Mojave Desert, where forests of the Joshua tree are found. An entrance fee of $10 per vehicle is charged.

Park information is available from three visitor centers: Black Rock, Cottonwood, and Oasis. Cottonwood and Oasis Visitor Centers are open all year; Black Rock is closed during summer. The Oasis Visitor Center is located in Twentynine Palms.

There are nine campgrounds in Joshua Tree National Park. None have hookups for recreational vehicles.

- **Belle**: located about ten miles south of Twentynine Palms on Utah Trail, open all year, 18 RV/tent sites, pit toilets, 14 day maximum stay (30 days June through September), no fee, no water.

- **Black Rock**: located south of Yucca Valley on Joshua Lane, open all year, reservations accepted (1-800-365-2267), 100 RV/tent sites, $10 per night, water and flush toilets available, 14 day maximum stay (30 days June to October), 35-foot RV length limit, nature trails, dump station, visitor center at campground, horse camp available ($10 per night).

- **Cottonwood**: located on Cottonwood Spring Road about seven miles north of I-10, open year-round, 62 sites, $10 per night, water, flush toilets, dump station, Loop "B" of campground closed in summer, 14 day maximum stay

(30 days June through September).

- **Hidden Valley**: located 14 miles southeast of Joshua Tree along Park Boulevard, open all year, 45 sites, no fee, no water, pit toilets, 14 day maximum stay (30 days June to October).

- **Indian Cove**: located about five miles west of Twentynine Palms and three miles south of CA 62 on Indian Cove Road, open all year, reservations accepted (1-800-365-2267), 101 RV/tent sites, no water, pit toilets, $10 per night, 14 day maximum stay (30 days June through September).

- **Jumbo Rocks**: located 11 miles south of Twentynine Palms along Park Boulevard, open all year, 125 sites, no fee, no water, pit toilets, 14 day maximum stay (30 days June through September).

- **Ryan**: located 16 miles southeast of Joshua Tree off Park Boulevard, open all year, 31 sites, no fee, no water, pit toilets, 14 day maximum stay, horse camp available.

- **Sheep Pass**: located south of Twentynine Palms and west of Jumbo Rocks Campground off Park Boulevard, group camping only, open all year, reservations accepted (1-800-365-2267), no water, six group sites, pit toilets, $25 to $35 fee.

- **White Tank**: located south of Belle Campground and about 11 miles south of Twentynine Palms, open all year, 15 sites, no fee, no water, pit toilets, 14 day maximum stay.

Lassen Volcanic National Park

PO Box 100
Mineral, CA 96063
Phone: 530-595-4444
Fax: 530-595-3262

Lassen Volcanic National Park is in northern California, about 60 miles east of Redding. The park covers 106,372 acres and receives around 350,000 visitors each year. All four types of volcanoes in the world can be found in the park. An entrance fee of $10 per vehicle is charged. The park pass is good for seven days.

The park's headquarters is located in Mineral; information and publications are available year-round. Information is also available from the visitor center located near the northern entrance to the park and from the Southwest Information Station, at the park's southern entrance.

Lassen Volcanic National Park has eight camping areas. Campsites are available on a first-come, first-served basis; no reservations are accepted. Backcountry camping is permitted.

- **Butte Lake**: located about 17 miles from Old Station and six miles south of CA 44 via Forest Service Road 32N21, open mid-June to late September, accommodates RVs up to 35 feet long, 101 sites, $14 per night, boat launch, 14 day maximum stay, bear-proof boxes available.

- **Crags**: located five miles east of Manzanita Lake along CA 89, open July to early September, 45 sites, 35-foot RV length limit, $12 per night, potable water, bear-proof boxes available, 14 day maximum stay.

- **Juniper Lake**: located on the east shore of Juniper Lake about 13 miles north of Chester, access road is rough and not recommended for RVs, open July through September, 18 sites, $10 per night, swimming, bear-proof boxes available, 14 day maximum stay.

- **Manzanita Lake**: located adjacent to and south of Manzanita Lake off CA 89, open late May to late September, accommodates RVs up to 35 feet long, 179 sites, $16 per night, dump station, potable water, boat launch, fishing, swimming, pay phone, food, gift shop, showers, laundromat, bear-proof boxes available, 14 day maximum stay.

- **Southwest Walk-In**: located near the Southwest Entrance Station, open all year, no RV sites but RVs may park overnight in the Lassen Chalet parking lot for $10 per night, 21 tent sites, potable water and flush toilets available late May to late September, $14 per night, 14 day maximum stay.

- **Summit Lake North**: located off CA 89 about 12 miles southeast of Manzanita Lake, open July and August, 46 sites, 35-foot RV length limit, $16 per night, potable water, swimming, 14 day maximum stay.

- **Summit Lake South**: located off CA 89 about 12 miles southeast of Manzanita Lake, open July through September, 48 sites, $14 per night, potable water, swimming, 14 day maximum stay.

- **Warner Valley**: located about 17 miles north of Chester via Warner Valley Road that is not recommended for RVs, open June to October, 18 sites, $14 per night, potable water, fishing, bear-proof boxes available, 14 day maximum stay.

Lava Beds National Monument

1 Indian Well Headquarters
Tulelake, CA 96134
Phone: 530-667-2282 or 530-667-2282 ext 232
Fax: 530-667-2737

Lava Beds National Monument is in northeast California about 65 miles west of Alturas. Cinder cones, lava flows, and numerous lava tube caves characterize its 46,500 acres. It was designated a national monument in 1925. The park is open all year. An entrance fee of $10 is charged.

Information is available from the visitor center located in the Indian Wells Campground. It is open from 8:00 a.m. to 6:00 p.m. during summer and to 5:00 p.m. the rest of the year. It is closed on Thanksgiving and Christmas. Exhibits introduce you to the features in the monument.

There is only one campground available to visitors. Campsites are available on a first-come, first-served basis. The National Park Service describes the RV sites as suitable for "small to medium-sized RVs." One campsite is accessible to the handicapped.

- **Indian Wells**: located west of CA 139 via CR 97 and Lava Beds National Monument Road, open all year, 40 RV/tent sites, $10 per night, drinking water available in summer, flush toilets, 14 day maximum stay.

Mojave National Preserve

222 E Main St, Ste 202
Barstow, CA 92311
Phone: 760-255-8800 or 760-733-4040
Fax: 760-255-8809

Mojave National Preserve is in southeast California. It was established in 1994 and covers 1.6 million acres. The area ranges from creosote bush flats in low areas to pinyon pine and juniper woodlands at higher elevations. The preserve is open year-round. No entrance fee is charged.

Maps and brochures are available from the Baker Information Center at 72157 Baker Boulevard in Baker. The information center is open year-round. Information is also available from the Hole-in-the-Wall Ranger Station, 20 miles north of I-40 via Essex and Black Canyon Roads. The ranger station is staffed on weekends.

There are two campgrounds in the preserve. Campsites are available on a first-come, first-served basis. Backcountry camping is allowed as long as your campsite is more than one-half mile from any road or water source.

- **Hole-in-the-Wall**: located ten miles north of I-40 via Essex Road and Black Canyon Road, open all year, 35 RV/tent sites, two walk-in tent sites, $12 per night, picnic tables, fire rings, drinking water on a limited basis, dump station, pit toilets.

- **Mid Hills**: located about 30 miles north of I-40 via Essex Road and Black Canyon Road, open all year, 26 sites, $12 per night, not recommended for motorhomes and vehicles pulling trailers, picnic tables, fire rings, pit toilets, drinking water on a limited basis.

Point Reyes National Seashore

Superintendent
Point Reyes, CA 94956
Phone: 415-464-5100
Fax: 415-663-8132

Point Reyes National Seashore is in northern California about 22 miles north of San Francisco. The 65,300-acre area was established in 1962. It remains open all year. There is no entrance fee.

Information is available from three visitor centers. Bear Valley Visitor Center is the park's primary visitor center and is located off Bear Valley Road north of Olema. It remains open all year between 9:00 a.m. and 5:00 p.m. It is closed Christmas Day. Kenneth C. Patrick Visitor Center is 30 minutes from Bear Valley on Drakes Beach off Sir Frances Drake Boulevard. It is open all year on weekends and holidays. Lighthouse Visitor Center is 45 minutes from Bear Valley on the Point Reyes Headlands, at the end of Sir Frances Drake Boulevard. It is open Thursday through Monday year-round.

There are four hike-in campgrounds in the park. Camping is restricted to these campgrounds. Permits are required and are available at the Bear Valley Visitor Center. Camping is limited to a total of four nights. Reservations are strongly recommended and can be made up to three months in advance by calling 415-663-8054. Boat-in only camping is permitted on Tomales Bay.

- **Coast Camp**: open all year, picnic tables, food storage locker, charcoal grills, pit toilets, drinking water, $12 per night. The shortest hike to the camp is 1.8 miles. No dogs allowed.

- **Glen Camp**: open all year, picnic tables, food storage locker, charcoal grills, pit toilets, drinking water, $12 per night. The shortest hike to this camp is five miles. No dogs allowed.

- **Sky Camp**: open all year, picnic tables, food storage locker, charcoal grills, pit toilets, drinking water, 12 sites, $12 per night. The shortest hike to this camp is 1.3 miles. No dogs allowed.

- **Wildcat Camp**: open all year, picnic tables, food storage locker, charcoal grills, pit toilets, drinking water, $12 per night. No dogs allowed.

Redwood National and State Parks

1111 2nd St
Crescent City, CA 95531
Phone: 707-464-6101
Fax: 707-464-1812

Redwood National and State Parks are located in northwest California. The area is a cooperative management effort between the National Park Service and California Department of Parks and Recreation. Three California state parks and the National Park Service unit make up this area that protects 45 percent of all the old-growth redwood forest remaining in California. There is no entrance fee charged for the National Park Service unit. A fee is charged to enter the state parks.

Information is available from three visitor centers and two information centers. Jedediah Smith Visitor Center is on US 101 at Hiouchi. It is open mid-May through September from 9:00 a.m. to 5:00 p.m. Prairie Creek Visitor Center is just of US 101 along Newton B. Drury Scenic Parkway. It remains open all year. Thomas H. Kuchel Visitor Center is along US 101 at Orick. It is open all year from 9:00 a.m. to 5:00 p.m. Crescent City Information Center is at 1111 Second Street in Crescent City. It is open year-round. Hiouchi Information Center is open mid-June to mid-September and is on US 199 at Hiouchi.

There are four campgrounds available to visitors. All are managed by the State of California. Please note that Golden Age and Golden Access Passports may not be honored at these campgrounds. California does have a similar discount program, however. Other campgrounds can be found in the surrounding national forest.

- **Elk Prairie**: located off US 101 on Newton B. Drury Scenic Parkway in Prairie Creek Redwoods State Park, open all year, 75 RV/tent sites, $16 per night, 27-foot RV length limit (24 feet for trailers), 14 day maximum stay, showers, restrooms, picnic area, trails, dump station, fire pits, bearproof lockers, handicap access, no hookups, reservations accepted (800-444-7275).

- **Gold Bluffs Beach**: located in Prairie Creek Redwoods State Park at the end of Davison Road off US 101, open all year, 25 RV sites, 29 tent sites, RVs limited to 24 feet long and 8 feet wide, restrooms, solar showers, fire pits, $16 per night, 14 day maximum stay, no reservations accepted.

- **Jedediah Smith**: located nine miles east of Crescent City along US 199 in Jedediah Smith Redwoods State Park, open all year, 106 RV/tent sites, 36-foot RV length limit (31 feet for trailers), restrooms, showers, dump station, bearproof lockers, fire pits, $16 per night, 14 day maximum stay, reservations accepted (800-444-7275).

- **Mill Creek**: located seven miles south of Crescent City off US 101 in Del Norte Coast Redwoods State Park, open April through September, 145 RV/tent sites, $16 per night, 45-foot RV length limit (35 feet for trailers), restrooms, showers, dump station, bearproof lockers, fire pits, handicap access, trails, 14 day maximum stay, reservations accepted (800-444-7275).

Santa Monica Mountains National Rec. Area

401 W Hillcrest Dr
Thousand Oaks, CA 91360
Phone: 805-370-2300 or 805-370-2301
Fax: 805-370-1850

Santa Monica Mountains National Recreation Area is located in southern California, northwest of Los Angeles. The area encompasses 150,000 acres of mountains, canyons, woodlands, and miles of beach. It was established in 1978 and is managed cooperatively by federal, state, and local park agencies. There is no entrance fee.

Information is available from the National Park Service Visitor Center located at 401 West Hillcrest Drive in Thousand Oaks. The center is open daily from 9:00 a.m. to 5:00 p.m. It closes on Thanksgiving, Christmas, and New Year's Day. Exhibits feature interactive displays and historical artwork.

There are four camping areas in the park. All are managed by the State of California. Please note that Golden Age and Golden Access Passports may not be honored at these areas. California does have a similar discount program, however.

- **Canyon Family Camp**: located in Leo Carrillo State Park west of Malibu along CA 1, open all year, 138 RV/tent sites, $16 per night, drinking water, flush toilets, showers, dump station, fire rings, seven day maximum stay (15 days October through May), 31-foot RV length limit, reservations accepted (800-444-7275).

- **Big Sycamore Canyon Family Camp**: located in Point Mugu State Park, open all year, 58 RV/tent sites, $16 per night, drinking water, flush toilets, showers, dump station, fire rings, reservations accepted (800-444-7275), seven day maximum stay (15 days October through May).

- **Thornhill Broome Family Camp**: located in Point Mugu State Park, open all year, 68 RV/tent sites, $16 per night, drinking water, pit toilets, fire rings, seven day maximum stay (15 days October through May), reservations accepted (800-444-7275).

- **Malibu Creek Family Camp**: located in Malibu Creek State Park, open all year, 63 RV/tent sites, $16 per night, drinking water, flush toilets, showers, dump station, fire rings, reservations accepted (800-444-7275), seven day maximum stay (15 days October through May).

Sequoia & Kings Canyon National Parks

47050 Generals Highway
Three Rivers, CA 93271
Phone: 559-565-3341
Fax: 559-565-3730

Sequoia and Kings Canyon National Parks are two
separate parks managed as one. Together, the parks preserve immense
mountains, deep canyons, and towering sequoia trees. Sequoia National
Park contains the highest mountain in the lower 48 states, Mount
Whitney. Kings Canyon National Park is home to North America's
deepest canyon. An entrance fee of $10 for vehicles is charged and is
good for seven days.

Park information is available from three visitor centers. Grant Grove
Visitor Center in Kings Canyon National Park is three miles east on
CA 180 from the Big Stump Entrance Station. The Foothills Visitor
Center and Lodgepole Visitor Center are located in Sequoia National
Park. The first is on Generals Highway about one mile from the park
entrance. The latter is on Lodgepole Road just off Generals Highway
about 21 miles from the park entrance.

A total of 14 campgrounds are available. Most have bear-proof food
storage that must be used. Reservations are accepted for campsites in
Lodgepole and Dorst campgrounds in Sequoia National Park; call 1-
800-365-2267. All other campsites are available on a first-come, first-
served basis. RVs are not permitted at Atwell Mill, Buckeye Flat, and
Cold Spring campgrounds in Sequoia National Park. Many sites at the
remaining campgrounds are not suitable for RVs. A limited number of
sites can accommodate RVs over 30 feet long. No hookups are available
in any of the campgrounds.

Campgrounds in Kings Canyon National Park are as follows:

- **Azalea**: open year-round, in the Grant Grove area 3.5 miles from park
  entrance, 113 sites, $18 per night, drinking water, tables, fire grills, flush
  toilets, pay phone, limited RV space, 14 day maximum stay mid-June to

mid-September. Near visitor center, market, restaurant, gift shop, and showers.

- **Canyon View**: open as needed May to October, in Cedar Grove area near Kings River, 37 sites, $18 per night, flush toilets, pay phone, drinking water, tables, fire grills, 14 day maximum stay mid-June to mid-September. Nearby restaurant, market, showers, laundry, and horseback riding.

- **Crystal Springs**: open late May to mid-September, in the Grant Grove area four miles from the park entrance, 63 sites, $18 per night, drinking water, tables, fire grills, flush toilets, pay phone, 14 day maximum stay mid-June to mid-September. Near visitor center, market, post office, gift shop, and restaurant.

- **Moraine**: open as needed May to October, in the Cedar Grove area down in the canyon along Kings River, 120 sites, $18 per night, flush toilets, fire grills, tables, drinking water, 14 day maximum stay mid-June to mid-September. Near restaurant, pay phone, market, showers, laundry, and horseback riding.

- **Sentinel**: open late April to mid-November, in the Cedar Grove area, 83 sites, $18 per night, flush toilets, fire grills, tables, drinking water, 14 day maximum stay mid-June to mid-September. Near restaurant, market, pay phone, showers, laundry, and horseback riding.

- **Sheep Creek**: open as needed May to October, in the Cedar Grove area down in the canyon near Kings River, 111 sites, $18 per night, flush toilets, fire grills, tables, drinking water, 14 day maximum stay mid-June to mid-September. Near restaurant, market, pay phone, showers, laundry, and horseback riding.

- **Sunset**: open late May to mid-September, in the Grant Grove area three miles from park entrance, 200 sites, $18 per night, drinking water, tables, fire grills, flush toilets, pay phone, 14 day maximum stay mid-June to mid-September. Near visitor center, market, post office, gift shop, showers, and restaurant.

Campgrounds found in Sequoia National Park are as follows:

- **Atwell Mill**: open late May through October, located in the Mineral King area 19 miles from CA 198, access road is not recommended for RVs, campground does not accommodate RVs, 23 tent sites, $12 per night, pit toilets, pay phone, fire grills, tables, drinking water, 14 day maximum stay mid-June to mid-September. Near Silver City Resort with restaurant, gifts, supplies, gas, and showers.

- **Buckeye Flat**: open late spring to Labor Day, located off Generals Highway four miles from park entrance and 12 miles from Giant Forest, 28 tent sites, $18 per night, flush toilets, fire grills, drinking water, tables, 14 day maximum stay mid-June to mid-September.

- **Cold Springs**: open late May through October, located 23 miles from CA 198 up the steep and narrow Mineral King Road, access road not suitable for RVs, campground does not accommodate RVs, 40 tent sites, $12 per night, pit toilets, pay phone, fire grills, tables, drinking water, 14 day maximum stay mid-June to mid-September. Near Silver City Resort with restaurant, gifts, supplies, gas, and showers.

- **Dorst**: located 12 miles north of Giant Forest on Generals Highway, open late May to early September, reservations accepted (800-365-2267), 204 sites, $20 per night, flush toilets, dump station, pay phone, fire grills, tables, drinking water, 14 day maximum stay mid-June to mid-September.

- **Lodgepole**: located off Generals Highway two miles north of Giant Forest and 21 miles from park entrance, open all year, reservations accepted (800-365-2267), $20 per night May through September, $18 per night otherwise, 214 sites, flush toilets, dump station, pay phone, tables, drinking water, fire grills, 14 day maximum stay mid-June to mid-September. Near restaurant, market, gift shop, laundry, and showers.

- **Potwisha**: located four miles from park entrance along CA 198, open all year, 43 sites, $18 per night, flush toilets, dump station, pay phone, fire grills, tables, drinking water, 14 day maximum stay mid-June to mid-September.

- **South Fork**: on South Fork Drive 13 miles southeast of Three Rivers off CA 198, open all year, not recommended for RVs, 13 sites, $12 per night May through October, no fee rest of year, no drinking water, pit toilets, fire grills, tables, 14 day maximum stay mid-June to mid-September.

Whiskeytown National Recreation Area

PO Box 188
Whiskeytown, CA 96095
Phone: 530-242-3400 or 530-246-1225
Fax: 530-246-5154

Whiskeytown National Recreation Area is in northern California west of Redding. The park was established in 1972 and covers 42,500 acres. Features include mountainous backcountry, a large reservoir, and remains of buildings built during the Gold Rush. The park is accessible year-round. A daily vehicle entrance fee of $5 is charged.

Information is available from the Whiskeytown Visitor Center located along CA 299 about eight miles west of Redding. The center is open all year. Summer hours are 9:00 a.m. to 6:00 p.m. Hours for the rest of the year are 10:00 a.m. to 4:00 p.m. It closes on Thanksgiving, Christmas, and New Year's Day. Three exhibits depicting the California Gold Rush and a wide selection of books are among the center's features.

There are two developed campgrounds within Whiskeytown National Recreation Area. Numerous primitive tent-only campsites are scattered throughout the area. These are available on a first-come, first-served basis and can only be accessed by traveling on dirt roads; some require the use of four-wheel drive vehicles. Summer camping fee is $10 per night; winter, $5 per night. The developed campgrounds are listed below.

- **Brandy Creek**: located five miles off CA 299 along Kennedy Drive, open all year, 37 RV sites, self-contained RVs only, $14 per night in summer, $7 per night in winter, 14 day maximum stay, restrooms, dump station, public phone. Sites are available first-come, first served only; no reservations accepted.

- **Oak Bottom**: located 13 miles west of Redding on CA 299, open all year, 100 RV sites ($14 per night), 300 tent sites ($16-18 per night), reservations accepted during summer season (800-365-2267), restrooms, showers, dump station, phone, 14 day maximum stay. During winter, sites are available on a first-come, first-served basis only. Winter rates: $8 per night for tent sites and $7 per night for RV sites.

Yosemite National Park

PO Box 577
Yosemite National Park, CA 95389
Phone: 209-372-0200
Fax: 209-372-0220

Yosemite National Park is in central California, about 100 miles east of Modesto. The park encompasses beautiful mountain and valley scenery in the Sierra Nevada Mountains. An entrance fee of $20 per vehicle is charged. The park remains open year-round but some roads may close due to snow.

Visitor centers are located in Yosemite Valley (open year-round) and Tuolumne Meadows (summer only). Information stations are located in Wawona and Big Oak Flat. Both are open spring through fall.

There are 13 campgrounds in Yosemite National Park. Seven accept reservations up to five months in advance. Backcountry camping is allowed but a permit is required (available free from the visitor centers). Campgrounds are also in national forest land surrounding the park.

- **Bridalveil Creek**: 27 miles from Yosemite Valley off Glacier Point Road, open July to early September, sites available on a first-come first-served basis, 14 day maximum stay, 35-foot RV length limit, 110 RV/tent sites, $12 per night, water, flush toilets, no hookups.

- **Camp 4**: walk-in campsites in the Yosemite Valley area, open year-round, 35 sites available on a first-come first-served basis, $5 per person, drinking water, flush toilets. Sites are rented on a per person basis and up to six people will be placed in each campsite regardless of the number of people in your party.

- **Crane Flat**: on Big Oak Flat Road (CA 120) 17 miles west of Yosemite Valley, open June to September, reservations required (800-436-7275), 166 RV/tent sites, $18 per night, water, flush toilets, 14 day maximum stay,

35-foot RV length limit, no hookups.

- **Hodgdon Meadow**: on Big Oak Flat Road (CA 120) 25 miles west of Yosemite Valley, open year-round, reservations required in summer (800-436-7275), 105 sites, $18 per night mid-April to mid-October, $12 per night rest of year, drinking water, flush toilets, 14 day maximum stay, 35-foot RV length limit, no hookups.

- **Lower Pines**: in the Yosemite Valley area, open March through October, reservations required (800-436-7275), seven day maximum stay in summer, 60 sites, $18 per night, water, flush toilets, dump station nearby, showers and laundry nearby, 35-foot RV length limit, no hookups.

- **North Pines**: in the Yosemite Valley area, open April through September, reservations required (800-436-7275), seven day maximum stay in summer, 81 sites, $18 per night, drinking water, flush toilets, dump station nearby, shower and laundry facilities nearby, 35-foot RV length limit, no hookups.

- **Porcupine Flat**: on Tioga Pass Road about 30 miles east of Big Oak Flat Entrance, open July to early September, campsites available on a first-come first served basis, 52 sites, $8 per night, pit toilets, 14 day maximum stay, 35-foot RV length limit, no hookups, no drinking water.

- **Tamarack Flat**: about 15 miles east of Big Oak Flat Entrance off Tioga Pass Road, open June to early September, 52 sites available on first-come first-served basis, $8 per night, 14 day maximum stay, pit toilets, no drinking water, no hookups. Three-mile access road is not suitable for trailers or large RVs, inquire at visitor center.

- **Tuolumne Meadows**: along CA 120 (Tioga Pass Road) about six miles west of Tioga Pass Entrance, open July through September, 304 sites, reservations required for half of the sites (800-436-7275), drinking water, flush toilets, dump station nearby, $18 per night, 14 day maximum stay, 35-foot RV length limit, no hookups, showers nearby.

- **Upper Pines**: in the Yosemite Valley area, open year-round, reservations required (800-436-7275), seven day maximum stay in summer, 238 sites, $18 per night, water, flush toilets, dump station, showers and laundry nearby, 35-foot RV length limit, no hookups.

- **Wawona**: off CA 41 about eight miles north of Fish Camp, open year-round, seven day maximum stay in summer, 93 RV/tent sites, $18 per night, water, flush toilets, reservations required in summer (800-436-7275), 35-foot RV length limit, no hookups, dump station nearby.

- **White Wolf**: one mile north of Tioga Pass Road about 22 miles east of Big Oak Flat Entrance, open June through early September, 74 RV/tent sites available on a first-come first-served basis, $12 per night, drinking water, flush toilets, 14 day maximum stay, 35-foot RV length limit, no hookups.

- **Yosemite Creek**: south of Tioga Pass Road about 30 miles east of Big Oak Flat Entrance, open July to early September, 75 sites available on a first-come first-served basis, $8 per night, pit toilets, 14 day maximum stay, no drinking water and no hookups. Five-mile access road not suitable for vehicles pulling trailers or RVs over 24 feet.

Colorado

1 Black Canyon of the Gunnison National Park
2 Colorado National Monument
3 Curecanti National Recreation Area
4 Dinosaur National Monument
5 Great Sand Dunes National Park & Preserve
6 Mesa Verde National Park
7 Rocky Mountain National Park

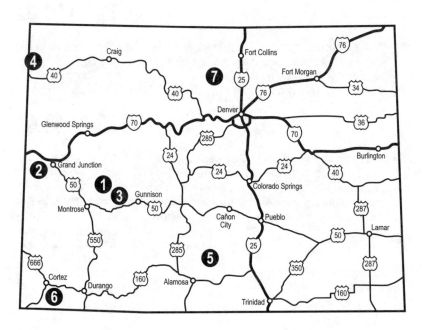

Activities Chart

Park	🚗	🚲	🥾	🐴	🏃	🏊	🐋	🏄	🏊	✈	🎿	⛴
1	•		•	•	•		•	•			•	•
2	•	•	•	•								
3	•		•	•	•	•	•	•	•	•	•	•
4	•	•	•		•		•	•			•	•
5	•	•	•		•		•				•	•
6		•		•							•	•
7	•	•	•	•	•		•				•	•

Black Canyon of the Gunnison National Park

102 Elk Creek
Gunnison, CO 81230
Phone: 970-641-2337 ext 205
Fax: 970-641-3127

Black Canyon of the Gunnison National Park is in western Colorado about 75 miles southeast of Grand Junction. It features narrow canyon walls that drop almost vertically for 2,000 feet to the Gunnison River. Numerous scenic overlooks are easily accessed by car or a short walk. A $7 entrance fee is charged that is good for seven days.

Information is available from the visitor center located on South Rim Drive about two miles from the south rim entrance. Features include exhibits and orientation programs. It remains open all year.

There are two campgrounds within the park. Sites in both are available on a first-come, first-served basis; reservations are not accepted. Water is available only from mid-May to mid-October.

• **North Rim**: located 11 miles south of Crawford on Black Canyon Road, open April to October, 13 sites, $10 per night, pit toilets, tables, grills, water in summer, no hookups, 14 day maximum stay, 35-foot RV length limit.

- **South Rim**: located 15 miles east of Montrose via CO 347, open April to October, 88 sites, $10 per night, electric hookups available in Loop B only ($15 per night), pit toilets, tables, grills, water in summer, 14 day maximum stay, 35-foot RV length limit.

Colorado National Monument

Fruita, CO 81521
Phone: 970-858-3617
Fax: 970-858-0372

Colorado National Monument is in west-central Colorado about 12 miles west of Grand Junction. It was established in 1911 and covers about 20,500 acres. Features include sheer-walled canyons, soaring arches, weird formations, dinosaur fossils, and remains of prehistoric Indian cultures. The park is open all year. An entrance fee of $5 per vehicle is charged.

Maps and brochures are available from the visitor center located four miles inside the park from the west entrance. It is open year-round between 9:00 a.m. and 5:00 p.m. Features include an audiovisual program, exhibits, and a bookstore.

There is one campground within the monument. Wood fires are prohibited. A maximum of seven people per site is allowed. All campsites are available on a first-come, first-served basis. Backcountry camping is permitted.

- **Saddlehorn**: located along the park road about four miles from the west entrance, open all year, 80 sites, $10 per night, flush toilets, drinking water, charcoal grills, picnic tables, no water in winter, 14 day maximum stay.

Curecanti National Recreation Area

102 Elk Creek
Gunnison, CO 81230
Phone: 970-641-2337
Fax: 970-641-3127

Curecanti National Recreation Area is in west-central Colorado between Montrose and Gunnison. Three lakes extend for 40 miles along the Gunnison River and the Black Canyon to form the heart of this recreation area. It was established in 1965 and encompasses nearly 42,000 acres. No entrance fee is charged. The park is open all year.

There are three visitor centers: Cimarron, Elk Creek, and Lake Fork. Cimarron is open mid-May through September. It is located near Cimarron, Colorado, 35 miles west of Gunnison on US 50. Elk Creek is 16 miles west of Gunnison on US 50. It is open mid-May through September. Lake Fork is 27 miles west of Gunnison off US 50 near Blue Mesa Dam. It is open only in summer.

There are nine campgrounds in the park. Campsites in all campgrounds are available on a first-come, first-served basis; no reservations accepted. Several boat-in campsites are scattered along the lakes.

- **Cimarron**: located 20 miles east of Montrose off US 50, open mid-April through September, 22 RV/tent sites, $10 per night, 30-foot RV length limit, 14 day maximum stay, picnic tables, fire grills, water, flush toilets, dump station, restaurant, visitor center at campground.

- **Dry Gulch**: located just north of US 50 about 17 miles west of Gunnison, open mid-May to mid-September, ten sites, $10 per night, picnic tables, fire grates, vault toilets, water, 14 day maximum stay.

- **East Portal**: located 17 miles east of Montrose via CO 347 and East Portal Road, open mid-May to mid-September, 15 sites, $10 per night, picnic tables, fire grates, vault toilets, water, 14 day maximum stay. RVs are not allowed because of the steep 16% grade and sharp, narrow curves on East Portal Road.

- **Elk Creek**: located 16 miles west of Gunnison on US 50, open all year, 163 RV/tent sites and 16 walk-in sites, $10 per night, water, showers, flush toilets, dump station, marina, boat ramp, restaurant, 30-foot RV length limit, 14 day maximum stay.

- **Gateview**: located at the extreme south end of the Lake Fork Arm of Blue Mesa Reservoir, open mid-May to mid-September, seven sites, no fee, picnic tables, fire grates, vault toilets, water. Access the campground from US 50 by traveling south on CO 149 about 25 miles, north on CR 25 for 2.5 miles, and north on CR 64 for four miles.

- **Lake Fork**: located 27 miles west of Gunnison off US 50 on CO 92, open mid-April through September, 82RV/tent sites and 5 walk-in sites, $10 per night, water, flush toilets, showers, marina, boat ramp, dump station, amphitheater, picnic tables, fire grills, 30-foot RV length limit, 14 day maximum stay.

- **Ponderosa**: located at the northwest end of the Soap Creek Arm of Blue Mesa Reservoir, open mid-April through September, 20 drive-in sites and nine walk-in sites, picnic tables, fire grates, vault toilets, drinking water, boat ramp, $10 per night, 14 day maximum stay. Campground is seven miles north of US 50 on Soap Creek Road, which can become muddy and hazardous when wet.

- **Red Creek**: located just north of US 50 about 19 miles west of Gunnison, open mid-May to mid-September, two sites, $10 per night, picnic tables, fire grates, vault toilets, water, 14 day maximum stay.

- **Stevens Creek**: located 12 miles west of Gunnison along US 50, open May through September, 54 RV/tent sites, $10 per night, water, vault toilets, amphitheater, boat ramp, 14 day maximum stay.

Dinosaur National Monument

4545 E Highway 40
Dinosaur, CO 81610
Phone: 970-374-3000 or 435-781-7700
Fax: 970-374-3003

Dinosaur National Monument is in northwest Colorado about 110 miles north of Grand Junction. Part of the monument is in northeastern Utah. The monument was established in 1915 and encompasses over 210,000 acres. Features include deep, narrow gorges, sandstone cliffs along the Green and Yampa Rivers, and one of the world's largest concentrations of fossilized dinosaur bones. The monument remains open year-round unless closed by adverse weather. An entrance fee of $10 is charged only in the Dinosaur Quarry area in Utah. The entrance fee is good for seven days.

Information is available from the visitor center located two miles east of Dinosaur, Colorado on US 40. Exhibits and a ten-minute orientation program provide information about the monument's scenic canyon country. The center is open all year. Summer hours are 8:00 a.m. to 6:00 p.m. Winter hours are 8:00 a.m. to 4:30 p.m. weekdays, closed on weekends and holidays. Information is also available from the Dinosaur Quarry Visitor Center north of Jensen, Utah. It also is open all year.

There are six campgrounds within the monument. Campsites are available on a first-come, first-served basis; reservations are not accepted. Most of the campgrounds do not fill up except on Labor Day and Memorial Day. Backcountry camping is allowed but a permit is required.

- **Deerlodge**: located 53 miles east of headquarters at the extreme eastern end of the monument, open all year, eight tent sites, no fee, vault toilets, picnic tables, fireplaces, no drinking water, 14 day maximum stay.

- **Echo Park**: located 38 miles north of headquarters at the end of Echo Park Road, open May through October, 17 tent sites, $8 per night, water, vault toilets, 14 day maximum stay. Access is dependent on weather; the last 13 miles of road are unpaved and impassable when wet. The road also requires a high-clearance vehicle.

- **Gates of Lodore**: located about 50 miles northwest of Maybell off CO 318, open all year, 17 sites, $8 per night, drinking water, vault toilets, picnic tables, fireplaces, 14 day maximum stay, 35-foot RV length limit.

- **Green River**: located five miles east of Dinosaur Quarry along UT 149, open April through September, 88 RV/tent sites, $13 per night, drinking water, restrooms, picnic tables, fireplaces, 14 day maximum stay, 35-foot RV length limit.

- **Rainbow Park**: located 23 miles northeast of Jensen off Island Park Road, open all year, two tent sites, no camping fee, vault toilet, picnic tables, fireplaces, no water, 14 day maximum stay. To reach the campground from Jensen, follow UT 149 to Brush Creek Road to Island Park Road. Some roads become impassable when wet.

- **Split Mountain**: located four miles east of Dinosaur Quarry, open all year, four tent sites, drinking water, restrooms, picnic tables, fireplaces, 14 day maximum stay. In summer, this campground is used only for group camping. Water is not available in winter.

Great Sand Dunes National Park & Preserve

11500 Highway 150
Mosca, CO 81146
Phone: 719-378-6300
Fax: 719-378-6310

Great Sand Dunes National Park and Preserve is in southern Colorado about 120 miles southwest of Pueblo. The 108,000-acre park features some of the largest and highest sand dunes in the United States. The park is open year-round. A $3 entrance fee is charged.

Information is available from the visitor center located along CO 150. It remains open all year. Features include a 15-minute video, exhibits, and bookstore.

There is one developed campground within the park. Campsites are available on a first-come, first-served basis. Backcountry camping is permitted at designated sites and in the dune wilderness; permits are required.

- **Pinyon Flats**: located at the end of CO 150, open all year, 88 RV/tent sites, $12 per night, fire grates, picnic tables, flush toilets, dump station, drinking water (April to October), 14 day maximum stay, 32-foot RV length limit.

Mesa Verde National Park

PO Box 8
Mesa Verde National Park, CO 81330
Phone: 970-529-4465
Fax: 970-529-4637

Mesa Verde National Park is in southwest Colorado about 40 miles west of Durango. Features of the park include Ancestral Puebloan structures and cliff dwellings dating from 550 A.D. to 1300 A.D. The park is open daily, year-round. An entrance fee of $10 for vehicles is charged that is good for seven days.

Information is available from the Far View Visitor Center located 15 miles from the park entrance. The visitor center is open 8:00 a.m. to 5:00 p.m. from early April to mid-October. Features include exhibits of historic Native American jewelry, pottery, and baskets. Tickets for cliff dwelling tours can be purchased here.

There is only one campground in the park. Please note that it is not operated by the National Park Service but is privately owned. Sites available on a first-come, first-served basis; reservations not accepted.

- **Morefield**: located four miles from the park entrance, open mid-April through mid-October, 435 RV/tent sites, 15 sites with hookups, $19 per night, $25 per night for sites with hookups, picnic tables, grills, drinking water, coin-operated showers, flush toilets, dump station, laundry facility, gas station, general store, 14 day maximum stay.

Rocky Mountain National Park

1000 Highway 36
Estes Park, CO 80517
Phone: 970-586-1206 or 970-586-1333
Fax: 970-586-1256

Rocky Mountain National Park is in north-central Colorado about 70 miles northwest of Denver. The park encompasses over 265,000 acres of some of the most beautiful mountain scenery in Colorado. Trail Ridge Road, an All-American Road National Scenic Byway, crosses the park and the Continental Divide. The road provides views of numerous mountain peaks stretching above 14,000 feet. An entrance fee of $15 is charged that is good for seven days.

Park information is available from six visitor centers. The Alpine Visitor Center is at Fall River Pass, at the junction of Trail Ridge and Fall River roads, four miles east of the Continental Divide. It is open mid-August to mid-October. Beaver Meadows Visitor Center remains open year-round and is on US 36, three miles from Estes Park at the park entrance. Fall River Visitor Center is on US 34 five miles west of Estes Park; it is open daily. Kawuneeche is one mile north of Grand Lake on US 34; it remains open all year. Lily Lake is on CO 7 six miles south of Estes Park; it is open during summer. Moraine Park is off Bear Lake Road about two miles from the Beaver Meadows entrance and is only open during summer.

There are five campgrounds within Rocky Mountain National Park. Reservations may be made for sites in Moraine Park and Glacier Basin by calling 800-365-2267. Quiet hours for all campgrounds are 8:00 p.m. to 8:00 a.m. No RV hookups or showers are available in any of the campgrounds.

- **Aspenglen**: located just inside the Fall River entrance on US 34 five miles west of Estes Park, open mid-May to late September, 54 sites, $18 per night, 7 day maximum stay, sites available first-come first-served; reservations not accepted, hiking trails, 30-foot RV length limit.

- **Glacier Basin**: located seven miles west of Beaver Meadows Visitor Center on Bear Lake Road, open late May to mid-September, 150 RV/tent sites, $18 per night, reservations required (800-365-2267), group sites available, 7 day maximum stay, 30-foot RV length limit (27 feet for trailers), flush toilets, dump station, phones.

- **Longs Peak**: located just off CO 7 nine miles south of Estes Park, open all year, 26 tent-only sites, $18 per night in summer, $12 per night rest of year, water in summer, first-come first-served; no reservations accepted, 3 day maximum stay in summer, 14 days rest of year.

- **Moraine Park**: seven miles west of Estes Park off Bear Lake Road, open all year, 247 RV/tent sites, $18 per night during summer, $12 per night when water is unavailable, reservations (800-365-2267) required in summer, first-come first-served rest of year, 32-foot RV length limit, 7 day maximum stay in summer, 14 day maximum stay rest of year, flush toilets, dump station, horseback riding nearby, hiking trails, campfire programs at amphitheater in summer.

- **Timber Creek**: located ten miles north of Grand Lake on US 34, 100 sites, open year-round on a first-come, first-served basis, $18 per night in summer, $12 per night when water is unavailable, flush toilets, dump station, 30-foot RV length limit, 7 day maximum stay in summer, 14 day maximum stay rest of year, campfire programs at amphitheater in summer.

Florida

1   Big Cypress National Preserve
2   Biscayne National Park
3   Canaveral National Seashore
4   Dry Tortugas National Park
5   Everglades National Park
6   Gulf Islands National Seashore

Activities Chart

Park	🚗	🚲	🥾	🐎	🚶	🛶	🚤	🏄	🏊	⛵	🎿	⛺
1	•	•	•		•		•	•		•		
2			•		•	•	•	•	•	•		
3			•	•	•	•	•	•	•	•		
4					•	•			•	•		
5	•	•			•	•	•			•		
6	•	•			•	•	•	•	•	•		

Big Cypress National Preserve

HCR 61 Box 110
Ochopee, FL 34141
Phone: 239-695-2000 or 239-695-1201
Fax: 239-695-3901

Big Cypress National Preserve is in southern Florida between Miami and Naples. The 729,000-acre area was set aside in 1974 to protect the Big Cypress Watershed. There is no entrance fee.

Information is available from the visitor center on US 41 (Tamiami Trail). It is open all year from 8:30 a.m. to 4:30 p.m. except on Christmas Day. Features include a 15-minute movie about the preserve, a wildlife exhibit, and book sales.

There is one developed and four primitive campgrounds within the preserve. Campsites are available on a first-come, first served basis. Bear Island, Midway, Mitchell's Landing, and Pinecrest are the four primitive campgrounds. All are open year-round. None have water or restrooms. The developed campground is described below.

- **Monument**: located along US 41, open all year, flush toilets, water, cold showers, dump station, no hookups, $14 per night.

Biscayne National Park

9700 SW 328th St
Homestead, FL 33033
Phone: 305-230-1144 or 305-230-7275
Fax: 305-230-1190

Biscayne National Park is in southern Florida, south of Miami. Ninety-five percent of the park is covered by water. A park concessionaire offers several ways to explore this park by providing glass bottom boat tours, snorkeling trips, dive trips, island excursions, and canoe or kayak rentals.

Park information is available from the Dante Fascell Visitor Center, located nine miles east of Homestead on SW 328th Street. The visitor center is open all year from 9:00 a.m. to 5:00 p.m. except on Christmas Day. Features include films, interpretive programs, a bookstore, picnic area, gift shop, restrooms, and a short walking trail.

Two campgrounds are located within the park: Boca Chita Key and Elliott Key. All campground sites are available on a first-come, first-served basis; no reservations are accepted. Quite hours are 10:00 p.m. to 6:00 a.m. Access to either campground is by boat only. To arrange for transportation, call the park's concessionaire at 305-230-1100. There is no trash service on the islands; all trash needs to be brought back with you to the mainland for disposal.

- **Boca Chita Key**: open all year, picnic tables, grills, saltwater restroom, no fresh water is available, 14 day maximum stay, $10 per night, $15 per night if you have a boat in the harbor.

- **Elliott Key**: open all year, picnic tables, grills, restrooms, drinking water, cold showers, trails, 14 day maximum stay, 40 sites, $10 per night, $15 per night if you have a boat in the harbor.

Canaveral National Seashore

308 Julia St
Titusville, FL 32796
Phone: 321-267-1110 or 321-867-4077
Fax: 321-264-2906

Canaveral National Seashore is situated on a barrier island in east-central Florida near Titusville. The 57,600-acre area preserves the natural beach, dune, marsh, and lagoon habitats for many species of birds. Kennedy Space Center occupies the southern end of the island. Temporary closure is possible due to launch-related activities. An entrance fee of $5 per day, per vehicle is charged.

Information may be obtained from the visitor center located nine miles south of New Smyrna Beach on FL A1A. The center is open daily year-round except on Christmas Day. Features include various displays, a book sales area, and a video that is shown on request.

There are no developed RV campgrounds in Canaveral National Seashore. Beach camping is permitted from November through April. Island Camping is permitted year-round on several islands in Mosquito Lagoon. Boats or canoes are required to get to these sites. No facilities are available. A camping permit is required; the cost is $10 per night. Permits are available at the information center. Reservations may be made by phone or in person up to seven days in advance.

Dry Tortugas National Park

PO Box 6208
Key West, FL 33041
Phone: 305-242-7700
Fax: 305-242-7711

Dry Tortugas National Park lies about 70 miles west of Key West. The area is known for its bird and marine life, and its legends of pirates and sunken gold. Fort Jefferson, the largest of the 19th century American coastal forts, is a central feature. The park is open all year and can only be reached by boat or plane. A $5 entrance fee is charged.

Information is available from the visitor center located inside Fort Jefferson on Garden Key. It has exhibits on the history of Fort Jefferson and a video describing the park's history and natural resources. The visitor center remains open year-round.

There is one primitive campground in Dry Tortugas National Park. Campers must bring all supplies including fresh water, fuel, ice, and food. All sites are available on a first-come, first-served basis; no reservations accepted. All trash must be carried out upon departure.

- **Garden Key**: open all year, located on the same island as Fort Jefferson a short walk from the public dock, 13 sites, 11 sites can accommodate up to six people or three tents each, $3 per person per night, picnic tables, grills, saltwater flush toilets located at dock. Vessels may anchor between sunset and sunrise in a designated anchorage area.

Note: Garden Key campground is currently closed due to a failure in the sewage system. As of November 2003, no re-opening date was known.

Everglades National Park

40001 State Road 9336
Homestead, FL 33034
Phone: 305-242-7700
Fax: 305-242-7728

Everglades National Park is in southern Florida about 50 miles southwest of Miami. It is the only subtropical preserve in North America. Ranger led walks and talks are offered year-round. Boat tours are also available. The park is open all year. An entrance fee of $10 per vehicle is charged and is valid for seven days.

Park information is available from five visitor centers. Ernest F. Coe Visitor Center is located at the main park entrance west of Homestead and Florida City. It is open all year and has educational displays, orientation films, and brochures. The Flamingo Visitor Center is 38 miles southwest of the main entrance at the southern end of the park. It is open during winter and intermittently during summer. Gulf Coast Visitor Center is open all year and is located in Everglades City, in the northwest corner of the park. Royal Palm is four miles west of the park's main entrance and is open all year. Shark Valley Information Center is open year-round and is located along US 41 (Tamiami Trail) on the northern border of the park.

There are two developed campgrounds within the park. Nearly 50 primitive camping areas are scattered throughout the park. Permits are required for wilderness camping.

- **Flamingo**: located at the end of the main park road in Flamingo, open all year, reservations accepted (800-365-2267), 234 drive-in sites and 44 walk-in sites, $14 per night, cold showers, two dump stations, picnic tables, grills, amphitheater, public telephone, no hookups, 30 day maximum stay, 14 day maximum stay December through March.

- **Long Pine Key**: located seven miles from main entrance, open all year, 108 RV/tent sites, $14 per night, reservations accepted (800-365-2267), 36-foot RV length limit, restrooms, drinking water, public phones, dump station, picnic area, amphitheater, hiking trails, no hookups.

Gulf Islands National Seashore

1801 Gulf Breeze Parkway
Gulf Breeze, FL 32563
Phone: 850-934-2600 or 228-875-9057
Fax: 850-932-9654

Gulf Islands National Seashore consists of 11 separate units stretching 150 miles from West Ship Island in Mississippi to the eastern tip of Santa Rosa Island in Florida. The 135,607-acre park was established in 1971. Features include white sand beaches, historic forts, and nature trails. An entrance fee of $8 per vehicle is charged. The entrance fee is valid for seven days.

Information is available from four visitor centers. Fort Barrancas Visitor Center is in Pensacola Naval Air Station, Florida. Fort Pickens Visitor Center is in Pensacola Beach, Florida. The park's headquarters can be found in Gulf Breeze at Naval Live Oaks. William M. Colmer Visitor Center is located in Ocean Springs, Mississippi. All four centers are open year-round except on Christmas Day.

There are two campgrounds available to visitors. Primitive camping is allowed on the eastern end of Perdido Key and on Horn, Petit Bois, and East Ship Islands.

- **Davis Bayou**: located in Ocean Springs, Mississippi two miles south of US 90, open all year, 51 RV/tent sites, $14 to $16 per night, all sites have electric and water hookups, hot showers centrally located, amphitheater, playground, nature trails, public phone, flush toilets, dump station, 14 day maximum stay. Campsites are available on a first-come, first-served basis.

- **Fort Pickens**: located on the west end of Santa Rosa Island about nine miles west of Gulf Breeze, open all year, 200 RV/tent sites with electric and water hookups, $20 per night, paved parking pads, reservations accepted (800-365-2267), picnic tables, grills, hot showers, nature trail, bike trail, dump station, 14 day maximum stay, 55-foot RV length limit.

Georgia

1   Cumberland Island National Seashore

Activities Chart

Park	🚙	🚴	🥾	🐴	🚶	〰️	⛵	🛶	🏊	✈️	⛷️	🛥️
1		•	•		•	•		•			•	

Cumberland Island National Seashore

PO Box 806
Saint Marys, GA 31558
Phone: 888-817-3421
Fax: 912-673-7747

Cumberland Island National Seashore is in southeast Georgia, seven miles east of Saint Marys. It was established in 1972 and encompasses 36,415 acres of land and water. The island is accessible by a concession operated passenger ferry. A day-use fee of $4 is charged in addition to ferry prices.

Visitors may wish to obtain information from the Mainland Visitor Center in Saint Marys. It remains open all year, except Christmas Day, between 8:15 a.m. and 4:30 p.m. A museum is nearby that contains a collection of artifacts from Cumberland Island.

Camping on Cumberland Island is limited to one developed and four primitive backcountry sites. All camping is limited to seven days and reservations are required. The backcountry sites range from 3.5 to nearly 11 miles from the ferry dock.

- **Backcountry**: open all year, no facilities, $2 per person per day, seven day maximum stay, drinking water should be treated, campfires not permitted, portable stoves suggested, reservations required.

- **Sea Camp**: open all year, $4 per person per day, restrooms, cold showers, drinking water, grills, fire rings, picnic tables, seven day maximum stay, reservations required.

Hawaii

1 Haleakala National Park
2 Hawaii Volcanoes National Park

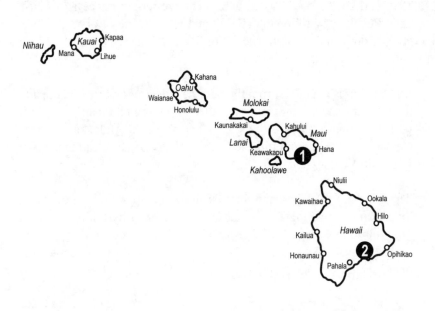

Activities Chart

Park	🚗	🚲	🥾	🐴	🚶	🏊	🐋	🏄	🏊	🪂	🏂	🛶
1			•	•	•				•			
2	•		•		•				•			

Haleakala National Park

PO Box 369
Makawao, HI 96768
Phone: 808-572-4400

Haleakala National Park preserves the volcanic landscape of the upper slopes of Haleakala on the island of Maui. The park was established in 1916 and covers over 30,000 acres. The western entrance is reached from Pukalani by following HI 377 and HI 378. Eastern access is via HI 31 from Hana. An entrance fee of $10 per vehicle is charged that is valid for seven days.

Information is available from the park headquarters located just inside the west entrance. It remains open all year between 8:00 a.m. and 4:00 p.m. Information may also be obtained from the Haleakala Visitor Center, near the summit of Haleakala. At the park's east entrance is the Kipahulu Visitor Center. It remains open all year.

There is one developed and three primitive campgrounds in the park. Two primitive campgrounds can only be reached by hiking to them. Only pit toilets are provided. Both require a free backcountry permit, which is available at park headquarters. Three wilderness cabins are also available; contact the park for more information.

- **Hosmer Grove**: located just inside the park's west entrance, open all year, picnic tables, grills, drinking water, pit toilets, two day maximum stay. Campsites are available on a first-come, first served basis. A self-guided nature trail begins and ends at the campground.

- **Kipahulu**: primitive campground located near the ocean at the park's east entrance, open all year, no drinking water, picnic tables, grills, pit toilets, two day maximum stay. Sites available on a first-come, first-served basis.

Hawaii Volcanoes National Park

PO Box 52
Hawaii National Park, HI 96718
Phone: 808-985-6000
Fax: 808-985-6004

Hawaii Volcanoes National Park is on the island of Hawaii about 28 miles southwest Hilo. It was established in 1916 and encompasses nearly 210,000 acres. Landscape features vary from sea level to the summit of the massive volcano, Mauna Loa at 13,677 feet. Over half of the park is designated wilderness and provides unusual hiking and camping opportunities. The park is open year-round. An entrance fee of $10 per vehicle is charged that is good for seven days.

Information is available from the Kilauea Visitor Center, located just inside the park entrance. It is open daily all year from 7:45 a.m. to 5:00 p.m. Videos highlighting the park's special features and current eruption are shown in the auditorium.

There are two drive-in campgrounds within the park. Campsites in both are available on a first-come, first-served basis. No camping fees are charged. Backcountry camping is by permit only.

- **Namakani Paio**: located along HI 11 about 31 miles from Hilo, open all year, restrooms, water, picnic tables, barbecue pits, seven day stay limit.

- **Kulanaokuaiki**: located about five miles down Hilina Pali Road, open all year, three sites, two are wheelchair accessible, barbecue grills, vault toilets, picnic tables, no water, seven day maximum stay.

Idaho

1   City of Rocks National Reserve
2   Craters of the Moon National Monument
3   Yellowstone National Park, *see Wyoming*

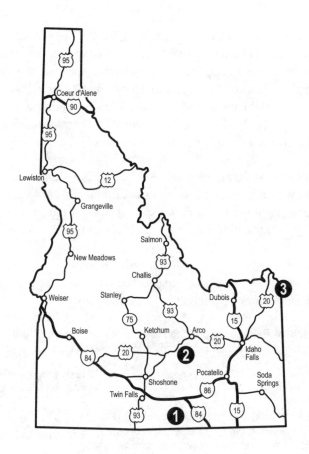

Activities Chart

Park												
1	•	•	•	•	•					•	•	•
2	•	•	•		•					•	•	

City of Rocks National Reserve

PO Box 169
Almo, ID 83312
Phone: 208-824-5519
Fax: 208-824-5563

City of Rocks National Reserve is in southern Idaho about 70 miles southeast of Twin Falls. The 14,107-acre park was established in 1988. Features include scenic granite spires and sculptured rock formations. Remnants of the California Trail are still visible in the area. There is no entrance fee.

Information is available from the visitor center in Almo. Brochures, climbing guides, historic trail information, camping information, books, and gifts are available. The center is open all year Monday through Friday between 8:00 a.m. and 4:30 p.m. It closes on holidays.

There are no developed campgrounds in City of Rocks. About 75 designated primitive campsites are scattered throughout the park; most are accessible from the road. Campsites are equipped with picnic tables and fire rings. Vault toilets are located throughout the preserve. Potable water is only available at the hand pump well located along Emery Canyon Road about one mile north of Bath Rock. All other water should be treated before using. The camping fee for one vehicle and one site is $7 per night. An additional $5 is charged for an extra vehicle. A maximum of two vehicles, eight people, and two tents are allowed at a single site. Reservations are not required but may be made by calling 208-824-5519.

Craters of the Moon National Monument

PO Box 29
Arco, ID 83213
Phone: 208-527-3257
Fax: 208-527-3073

Craters of the Moon National Monument is in central Idaho about 90 miles northeast of Twin Falls. It was established in 1924 and covers more than 53,000 acres. The park contains more than 25 volcanic cones and 60 different lava flows. The monument is accessible year-round. A $5 entrance fee per vehicle is charged that is valid for seven days.

Information is available from the Robert Limbert Visitor Center located just off US 20 about 25 miles northeast of Carey. It remains open all year. The center closes on holidays during winter. A museum located inside the visitor center has exhibits that explain the natural and cultural history of the area.

There is one campground in the monument. All campsites are available on a first-come, first-served basis; no reservations are accepted. Wood fires are not permitted. Quiet hours are 10:00 p.m. to 6:00 a.m. Water and other services are limited or unavailable October through May.

- **Craters of the Moon**: located near the visitor center, open all year, 52 RV/tent sites, $10 per night, picnic tables, grills, water, restrooms, 14 day maximum stay. The campground is not cleared of snow in winter.

Indiana

1   Indiana Dunes National Lakeshore

Activities Chart

Park												
1	•	•	•	•	•		•			•	•	•

Indiana Dunes National Lakeshore

1100 N Mineral Springs Rd
Porter, IN 46304
Phone: 219-926-7561 x225
Fax: 219-926-7561

Indiana Dunes National Lakeshore is in northwest Indiana just east of Gary. It runs for nearly 25 miles along southern Lake Michigan between Gary and Michigan City. The national lakeshore was established in 1966 and covers over 15,000 acres. Features include miles of beaches, sand dunes, woodland forests, an 1830's French Canadian homestead, and a working 1900-era farm combine. There is no entrance fee but a $6 user fee is charged in the West Beach area during summer.

Information is available from two visitor centers. Bailly/Chellberg Visitor Center is on Mineral Springs Road south of US 12, 1.5 miles west of IN 49. It is open daily during summer and on weekends in spring and fall. Dorothy Buell Memorial Visitor Center is open all year and is located on Kemil Road at US 12, about three miles east of IN 49.

There is one National Park Service campground. Campsites are available on a first-come, first-served basis; no reservations are accepted. Camping is also available in the nearby Indiana Dunes State Park.

- **Dunewood**: located off US 12 about five miles east of IN 49, open April through October, 54 drive-in sites, 25 walk-in sites, $15 per night, hot showers, picnic tables, fire grates, restrooms, no hookups, 14 day maximum stay, no RV length limit.

Kentucky

1 Big South Fork National River & Recreation Area, *see Tennessee*
2 Cumberland Gap National Historical Park
3 Mammoth Cave National Park

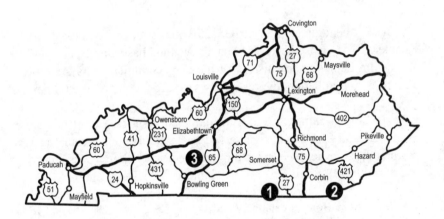

Activities Chart

Park											
2	•		•		•	•				•	
3		•		•	•	•	•			•	

Cumberland Gap National Historical Park

PO Box 1848
Middlesboro, KY 40965
Phone: 606-248-2817
Fax: 606-248-7276

Cumberland Gap National Historical Park is in southeast Kentucky, southwest Virginia, and northern Tennessee. The 20,454-acre park was established in 1940. This mountain pass developed into a main artery for settlers and was an important military objective in the Civil War. There is no entrance fee.

The park's headquarters is on US 25E just south of Middlesboro, Kentucky. The visitor center is open all year and has exhibits, artifacts, and a film depicting the history of the Gap. Summer hours are 8:00 a.m. to 6:00 p.m. Hours the rest of the year are 8:00 a.m. to 5:00 p.m.

One developed campground is available to visitors. Campsites are available on a first-come, first-served basis. Backcountry camping is permitted; campsites are located throughout the park. A free backcountry use permit is required, which is available at the visitor center.

- **Wilderness Road**: located in Virginia along US 58 two miles east of US 25E, open all year, 160 sites, $10 per night, 41 sites have electric hookups ($15 per night), hot showers, flush toilets, dump station, restrooms, drinking water, picnic tables, fire grates, amphitheater, 14 day maximum stay.

Mammoth Cave National Park

PO Box 7
Mammoth Cave, KY 42259
Phone: 270-758-2251
Fax: 270-758-2349

Mammoth Cave National Park is in central Kentucky about 30 miles northeast of Bowling Green. The park was established in 1941 to preserve the longest recorded cave system in the world. It also preserves the scenic river valleys of the Green and Nolin rivers. The park encompasses nearly 53,000 acres. There is no entrance fee but cave tour fees can range from $4 to $45.

Information is available from the visitor center located along South Entrance Road, north of Park City. The center is open all year but hours vary by season. Features include exhibits of cave exploration, films, and a bookstore.

There are two campgrounds within the park. Reservations accepted at Headquarters campground. Quiet hours are 10:00 p.m. to 6:00 a.m. Backcountry camping is allowed; a permit is required. Over a dozen campsites are scattered along the hiking trails.

- **Headquarters**: operated by concessionaire, located near the park's visitor center, open March through November, 109 RV/tent sites, $16 per night, reservations accepted (800-967-2283), dump station, picnic tables, fire grills, camp store, token-operated showers, flush toilets, laundry facilities, water, 14 day maximum stay.

- **Houchins Ferry**: primitive campground on the banks of Green River, located north of Brownsville along Houchins Ferry Road, 12 tent sites, $12 per night, picnic tables, fire grills, potable water, chemical toilets, 14 day maximum stay.

Maine

1   Acadia National Park

Activities Chart

Park											
1	•	•	•	•	•	•	•		•	•	•

Acadia National Park

PO Box 177
Bar Harbor, ME 04609
Phone: 207-288-3338
Fax: 207-288-8813

Acadia National Park is in southeast Maine about 20 miles south of Ellsworth. It was the first national park established east of the Mississippi. It encompasses 47,633 acres of granite-domed mountains, woodlands, lakes and ponds, and ocean shoreline. Some roads may close in winter; otherwise the park is accessible year-round. An entrance fee of $10 per vehicle is charged that is valid for seven days.

Information is available from the park headquarters located along ME 233 near Eagle Lake. It remains open all year. Information is also available from the Thompson Island Information Center located on the causeway at the head of Mount Desert Island on ME 3. The information center is open mid-May to mid-October. Hulls Cove Visitor Center is off ME 3 in Hulls Cove. It is open mid-April through October.

There are three campgrounds within the park. The campground on Isle au Haut is remote and inaccessible to automobiles. Campsites in Seawall are available on a first-come, first-served basis. In late July and August there is a great demand for campsites and lines form early each morning.

- **Blackwoods**: located on ME 3 five miles south of Bar Harbor, open all year, 181 tent sites, 84 RV/tent sites, 45 RV sites, $20 per night, reservations required May through October (800-365-2267), restrooms, water, dump station, picnic tables, fire rings, 14 day maximum stay, 35-foot RV length limit, facilities limited in winter, showers and supply stores nearby.

- **Seawall**: located on ME 102A four miles south of Southwest Harbor, open mid-May through September, 104 tent sites, 65 RV/tent sites, 42 RV sites, $14-20 per night, restrooms, water, dump station, picnic tables, fire rings, 14 day maximum stay, 35-foot RV length limit, facilities limited in winter, showers and supply stores nearby.

- **Duck Harbor**: located on Isle au Haut, inaccessible to automobiles, open mid-May to mid-October, five lean-to shelters, reservations required, $25 special use permit fee, picnic tables, fire rings, pit toilets, hand pump water, pack out trash, three night maximum stay mid-June to mid-September, five day maximum stay all other days.

Maryland

1 Assateague Island National Seashore
2 Catoctin Mountain Park
3 Chesapeake & Ohio Canal National Historical Park
4 Greenbelt Park

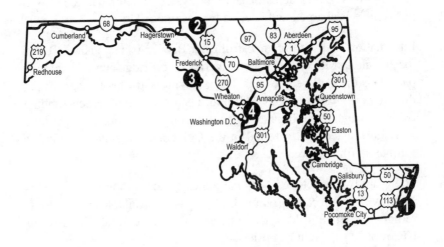

Activities Chart

Park	🚐	🚲	🥾	🐴	🏃	〰	🦆	🛶	🏊	⛷	🛷	
1	•	•		•		•	•	•	•			
2		•	•			•				•	•	
3	•	•	•	•	•	•	•			•	•	
4	•	•	•	•			•					

Assateague Island National Seashore

7206 National Seashore Ln
Berlin, MD 21811
Phone: 410-641-1441 or 757-336-6577

Assateague Island National Seashore is in southeast Maryland, eight miles south of Ocean City. A portion also extends into Virginia but is managed by the Fish and Wildlife Service as Chincoteague National Wildlife Refuge. The national seashore was established in 1965 and encompasses 39,723 acres of land and water. An entrance fee of $10 per vehicle is charged and is good for seven days.

Information may be obtained from the Barrier Island Visitor Center located along MD 611, before the Verrazzano Bridge entrance into the park. It is open all year, except Thanksgiving and Christmas, between the hours of 9:00 a.m. and 5:00 p.m. Features include beachcombing exhibits, educational brochures, nature films, and a marine aquarium. A visitor center is also found in the Chincoteague National Wildlife Refuge at Toms Cove.

There are two developed National Park Service campgrounds and six primitive walk-in campgrounds. Camping is not available in the wildlife refuge. The State of Maryland operates Assateague State Park, which has over 300 RV/tent campsites.

- **Developed**: one oceanside and one bayside campground located eight miles south of Ocean City via MD 611, open all year, 90 RV/tent sites, 63 tent sites, cold showers, chemical toilets, drinking water, picnic tables, fire grills, dump station, 14 day maximum stay, 40-foot RV length limit. Campsites are available first-come, first-served from mid-October through mid-May and cost $16 per night. Reservations are recommended from mid-May through mid-October, call 800-365-2267. Campsites during this time are $20 per night.

- **Primitive**: two oceanside and four bayside camping areas, open all year, chemical toilets, picnic tables. A backcountry permit is required ($5 fee).

Catoctin Mountain Park

6602 Foxville Rd
Thurmont, MD 21788
Phone: 301-663-9330
Fax: 301-271-2764

Catoctin Mountain Park is in northern Maryland about 20 miles east of Hagerstown. Originally established in 1936 as the Catoctin Recreational Demonstration Area, the 5,770-acre park was intended to provide recreational camps for federal employees. One of the camps eventually became the home of the Presidential retreat, Camp David. Although Camp David is not open or accessible to the public, the eastern hardwood forest of Catoctin Mountain Park has many other attractions for visitors. No entrance fee is charged.

Information is available from the visitor center located off Park Central Road about four miles west of Thurmont. The center is open all year between 10:00 a.m. and 4:30 p.m. A small exhibit area features native wildlife and cultural history.

There is one campground in the park, Owens Creek. Rustic cabin camping is available in Camp Misty Mount. There is a total of 28 cabins available to individuals or groups. A grill, fire ring, and picnic table are located outside each cabin. Drinking water, hot showers, and flush toilets are centrally located. Call 301-271-3140 for rental rates and more details.

- **Owens Creek**: located two miles north of MD 77 via Foxville Deerfield Road, open mid-April to mid-November, 51 sites, $16 per night, picnic tables, grill, flush toilets, hot showers, 50-foot RV length limit (22 feet for travel trailers), seven day maximum stay. Campsites are available on a first-come, first served basis; no reservations accepted.

Chesapeake & Ohio Canal Nat'l Historical Park

1850 Dual Hwy, Ste 100
Hagerstown, MD 21740
Phone: 301-739-4200
Fax: 301-739-5275

Chesapeake and Ohio Canal National Historical Park runs through central Maryland. Portions also extend into the District of Columbia and West Virginia. The park follows the route of the Potomac River for 184.5 miles from Washington, D.C. to Cumberland, Maryland. Hundreds of original structures, including locks, lockhouses, and aqueducts are among the park's features. An entrance fee of $5 per vehicle is charged at the Great Falls area. The entrance fee is valid for three days.

Six visitor centers are located throughout the park. All are open year-round but hours vary. The Brunswick Visitor Center is located at 40 West Potomac Street in Brunswick. Cumberland Visitor Center is in Cumberland at 13 Canal Street. Georgetown Visitor Center is located in Washington, D.C. at 1057 Thomas Jefferson Street NW. The Great Falls Tavern Visitor Center is at 11710 MacArthur Boulevard in Potomac, Maryland. Hancock Visitor Center is in Hancock, Maryland at 326 East Main Street. Williamsport Visitor Center is located at 205 West Potomac Street in Williamsport, Maryland. All have some type of exhibit on the canal's history as well as brochures.

There are three drive-in and 31 hiker/biker campgrounds. The hiker/biker campgrounds permit tent camping only and have pit toilets and pump well water. Length of stay is limited to one night in these campgrounds. The three drive-in campgrounds are described below.

- **Fifteen Mile Creek**: in Little Orleans east of Cumberland and south of I-68 via Orleans Road, open all year, ten RV/tent sites, $10 per night, primitive facilities, 14 day maximum stay in summer, 30 day maximum stay rest of year, 20-foot RV length limit. Campsites are available on a first-come, first-served basis only.

- **McCoys Ferry**: located 15 miles west of Hagerstown and south of I-70 via MD 56 and McCoys Ferry Road, open all year, 14 RV/tent sites, $10 per night, primitive facilities, no drinking water, 14 day maximum stay in summer, 30 day maximum stay rest of year, 20-foot RV length limit. Campsites are available on a first-come, first-served basis.

- **Spring Gap**: located eight miles south of Cumberland via MD 51, open all year, 20 RV/tent sites, $10 per night, primitive facilities, no drinking water, 14 day maximum stay in summer, 30 days rest of year, 20-foot RV length limit. Campsites are available on a first-come, first-served basis.

Greenbelt Park

6565 Greenbelt Rd
Greenbelt, MD 20770
Phone: 301-344-3948 or 301-344-3944
Fax: 301-344-1012

Greenbelt Park is in central Maryland about 25 miles southwest of Baltimore and 12 miles from Washington, D.C. It was established in 1950 and encompasses 1,176 acres. No entrance fee is charged.

Information is available from the park headquarters in Greenbelt along Greenbelt Road (MD 193). It is open Monday through Friday from 8:00 a.m. to 4:00 p.m. A ranger station is located at the entrance to the campground. Winter hours are 8:00 a.m. to 4:00 p.m. seven days a week.

There is one campground within the park. Campsite reservations can be made by calling 800-365-2267.

- **Greenbelt Park**: located off Park Central Road south of main entrance, open all year, 174 RV/tent sites, $14 per night, hot showers, restrooms, dump station, picnic tables, playground, public phones, hiking trails, near equestrian and bike trails, 14 day maximum stay, no RV hookups.

Massachusetts

1   Boston Harbor Islands National Recreation Area

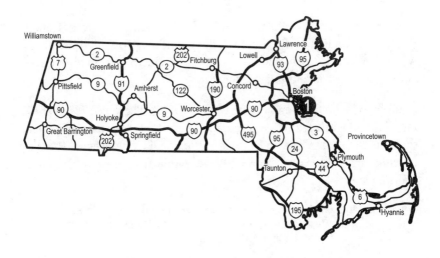

Activities Chart

Park												
1		•		•	•	•	•	•	•			

Boston Harbor Islands National Rec. Area

408 Atlantic Ave Ste 228
Boston, MA 02110
Phone: 617-223-8666 or 617-223-8667
Fax: 617-223-8671

Boston Harbor Islands National Recreation Area includes 30 islands situated within the Greater Boston shoreline. The islands are managed by a unique, 13-member partnership that includes the National Park Service and other public and private organizations. No entrance fee is charged. Passenger ferries connect to George's Island where water shuttles take visitors to other islands. The fare is $8 for adults, $7 for seniors, and $6 for children 4 to 12.

Information is available from the National Park Area Discovery Center located on Fan Pier at the United States Courthouse on South Boston's waterfront. Features include an interactive video, information desk, books and other island-related items for sale.

Camping reservations and permits are required. There is a reservation fee of $8.50 and a fee of $7 per night ($5 for Massachusetts residents) for individual campsites on Bumpkin Island and Grape Island. There is no camping fee beyond the $8.50 reservation fee for Lovell's Island and Peddock's Island.

- **Bumpkin Island**: located in Hingham Bay, open early May to September, ten individual tent sites, no drinking water, pit toilets, 14 day maximum stay, reservations required (877-422-6762).

- **Grape Island**: located in Hingham Bay, open early May to September, ten individual tent sites, pit toilets, no drinking water, 14 day maximum stay, reservations required (877-422-6762).

- **Lovell's Island**: located in Quincy Bay, open early May to September, ten individual tent sites, no drinking water, pit toilets, 14 day maximum stay, reservations required (877-422-6762).

- **Peddock's Island**: located in Quincy Bay, open early May to September, one central camping area (no individual sites), no drinking water, pit toilets, 14 day maximum stay, reservations required (877-422-6762).

Michigan

1   Isle Royale National Park
2   Pictured Rocks National Lakeshore
3   Sleeping Bear Dunes National Lakeshore

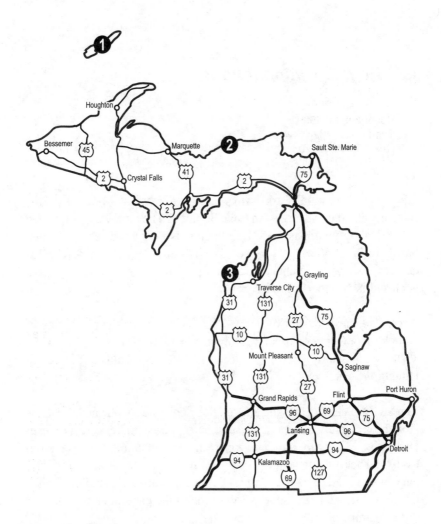

Activities Chart

Park	🚗	🚲	🚶	🐴	🚶	🏊	🐋	🏄	🏊	✈	⛷	🛶
1		•		•	•	•	•	•	•	•		
2		•		•	•	•	•	•	•	•	•	•
3	•		•		•	•	•	•	•	•	•	

Isle Royale National Park

800 E Lakeshore Dr
Houghton, MI 49931
Phone: 906-482-0984
Fax: 906-487-7170

Isle Royale National Park is in extreme northwest Michigan. This forested island is the largest in Lake Superior. The park was established in 1931 and encompasses 571,790 acres. No entrance fee is charged but there is a $4 per person, per day user fee. Vehicles and wheeled devices, except wheelchairs, are not allowed on Isle Royale. The park is closed November to mid-April.

Access to the island is by ferry. Visitors can park their vehicles in Houghton or Copper Harbor, Michigan or in Grand Portage, Minnesota. Visitors can also fly to the island via Isle Royale Seaplane Service in Houghton, Michigan.

Three visitor centers provide information about the island and its history. Houghton Visitor Center is located at 800 East Lakeshore Drive in Houghton, Michigan. It remains open all year but hours vary by season. Rock Harbor Visitor Center is located in the northeast section of the park in Rock Harbor. It is only open during summer. Windigo Visitor Center is located in the southwest section of the park and remains open during summer.

A total of 36 primitive campgrounds are available to visitors. Each may contain individual tent sites, three-sided shelters, or group sites. A permit, available free of charge, is required. Campgrounds are open mid-April through October. No facilities are available at the campgrounds but hot showers, groceries, and laundry facilities are available at Rock Harbor. Campsites are available only on a first-come, first-served basis. No camping fee is charged. Rock Harbor Lodge offers motel-style accommodations and self-contained cabins.

- **Beaver Island**: three shelters, three night maximum stay, accessed by boat and canoe or kayak, campstoves only, no fires.
- **Belle Isle**: one tent site, six shelters, five night maximum stay, fires permitted, boat and canoe or kayak access.
- **Birch Island**: one tent site, one shelter, three night stay, boat and canoe or kayak access, campstoves only, no fires allowed.
- **Caribou Island**: one tent site, two shelters, three night stay, boat and canoe or kayak access, fires permitted in community ring only.
- **Chickenbone East**: three tent sites, one group site, two night stay limit, accessed by trail and canoe or kayak, campstoves only.
- **Chickenbone West**: six tent sites, three group sites, two night stay limit, trail and canoe or kayak access, campstoves only.
- **Chippewa Harbor**: two tent sites, four shelters, one group site, boat and canoe or kayak access, trail access, campfires permitted, three night maximum stay.
- **Daisy Farm**: six tent sites, 16 shelters, three group sites, three night stay, boat and canoe or kayak access, trail access, campstoves only.
- **Desor North**: three tent sites, two night maximum stay, campstoves only, trail access.
- **Desor South**: seven tent sites, three group sites, two night stay, campstoves only, trail access.
- **Duncan Bay**: one tent site, two shelters, three night maximum stay, boat and canoe or kayak access, campfires allowed.
- **Duncan Narrows**: one tent site, two shelters, three night stay, boat and canoe or kayak access, campfires allowed.
- **Feldtmann Lake**: five tent sites, two group sites, two night maximum stay, campstoves only, trail and canoe or kayak access.
- **Grace Island**: two shelters, three night maximum stay, boat and canoe or kayak access, campstoves only.
- **Hatchet Lake**: five tent sites, three group sites, two night stay limit, campstoves only, trail access.
- **Hay Bay**: one tent site, three night stay limit, boat and canoe or kayak access, campstoves only.
- **Huginnin Cove**: five tent sites, three night stay limit, canoe or kayak access, trail access, campstoves only.
- **Intermediate Lake**: three tent sites, two night maximum stay, canoe or

kayak access, campstoves only.
- **Island Mine**: four tent sites, two group sites, three night stay, campfires allowed, trail access.
- **Lake Richie**: four tent sites, two group sites, two night stay limit, canoe or kayak access, trail access, campstoves only.
- **Lake Richey Canoe**: three tent sites, two night stay, canoe or kayak access, campstoves only.
- **Lake Whittlesey**: three tent sites, two night stay limit, canoe or kayak access, campstoves only.
- **Lane Cove**: five tent sites, three night maximum stay, canoe or kayak access, trail access, campstoves only.
- **Little Todd**: four tent sites, two night stay limit, campfires allowed, trail and canoe or kayak access.
- **Malone Bay**: five shelters, two group sites, three night maximum stay, boat and canoe or kayak access, trail access, campfires permitted.
- **McCargoe Cove**: three tent sites, six shelters, three group sites, three night stay, boat and canoe or kayak access, trail access, campfires permitted in community ring only.
- **Merritt Lake**: one tent site, one shelter, three night max stay, boat and canoe or kayak access, campstoves only.
- **Moskey Basin**: two tent sites, six shelters, two group sites, three night stay, boat and canoe or kayak access, trail access, campstoves only.
- **Pickerel Cove**: one tent site, two night maximum stay, canoe or kayak access, campstoves only.
- **Rock Harbor**: 11 tent sites, nine shelters, three group sites, one day stay limit, boat and canoe or kayak access, trail access, treated water supply, campstoves only.
- **Siskiwit Bay**: four tent sites, two shelters, three group sites, three night stay, boat and canoe or kayak access, trail access, campfires in community ring only.
- **Three Mile**: four tent sites, eight shelters, three group sites, one night stay limit, boat and canoe or kayak access, trail access, campstoves only.
- **Todd Harbor**: five tent sites, one shelter, three group sites, three night stay limit, boat and canoe or kayak access, trail access, campfires permitted in community ring only.
- **Tookers Island**: two shelters, three night stay limit, access by boat and canoe or kayak, campstoves only.
- **Washington Creek**: five tent sites, ten shelters, four group sites, three night stay, canoe or kayak access, trail access, treated water supply, campstoves only.
- **Wood Lake**: three tent sites, two night maximum stay, campstoves only, canoe or kayak access.

Pictured Rocks National Lakeshore

PO Box 40
Munising, MI 49862
Phone: 906-387-2607 or 906-387-3700
Fax: 906-387-4025

Pictured Rocks National Lakeshore is in northern
Michigan between Munising and Grand Marais. The park was
authorized in 1966 and encompasses 73,235 acres. Features include
sandstone cliffs, long beach strands, sand dunes, waterfalls, inland lakes,
wetlands, and hardwood forests.

Information is available in summer from the Grand Sable Visitor Center
located at E21090 County Road H58, one mile west of Grand Marais.
The Munising Falls Interpretive Center is open June through Labor
Day and is located at 1505 Sand Point Road in Munising. Information
can also be obtained year-round from the Pictured Rocks/Hiawatha
National Forest Visitor Center located in Munising at the junction of
Michigan Highway M28 and County Road H58.

There are three drive-in campgrounds within the park. All campsites
are available on a first-come, first-served basis. Several primitive hike-
in campgrounds are available and require a backcountry camping permit.

- **Hurricane River**: located off Alger County Road H58 12 miles west of
  Grand Marais, open mid-May through October, 21 RV/tent sites, $10 per
  night, picnic tables, fire grills, water, vault toilets, 14 day maximum stay.

- **Little Beaver Lake**: located 20 miles east of Munising off Alger County
  Road H58, open mid-May through October, eight sites, $10 per night, large
  RVs not recommended because of steep access road, nature trail, boat
  ramp, picnic tables, fire grills, water, vault toilets, 14 day maximum stay.

- **Twelvemile Beach**: located 12 miles west of Grand Marais off County
  Road H58, open mid-May through October, 37 RV/tent sites, $10 per night,
  picnic tables, fire grills, vault toilets, water, nature trail, 14 day stay limit.

Sleeping Bear Dunes National Lakeshore

9922 Front Street
Empire, MI 49630
Phone: 231-326-5134
Fax: 231-326-5382

Sleeping Bear Dunes National Lakeshore is in central Michigan about 24 miles west of Traverse City. The park encompasses a 35-mile stretch of Lake Michigan's eastern coastline. It was established in 1977. Features include hardwood forests, beaches, sand dunes, and steep bluffs. An entrance fee of $7 is charged that is valid for seven days.

Information is available from the Philip A. Hart Visitor Center located on State Highway M-72 in Empire. The center is open all year. Summer hours are 9:00 a.m. to 6:00 p.m. and 9:00 a.m. to 4:00 p.m. the rest of the year. Exhibits explain the history of the area. Information can also be obtained from the ranger stations in both campgrounds.

There are two developed campgrounds: D.H. Day and Platte River. Campsites at D.H. Day are available only on a first-come, first-served basis. Reservations can be made for campsites in Platte River by calling 800-365-2267. Backcountry camping is also available and requires the purchase of a backcountry permit ($5 per night).

- **D.H. Day**: located two miles west of Glen Arbor off MI 109, open April through November, 88 sites, $10 per night, 14 day stay limit, dump station, restrooms, water, public phone, amphitheater, handicap-accessible site.

- **Platte River**: located nine miles south of Empire via MI 22, open all year, 96 sites with 30-amp electric hookups ($19 per night), 53 sites without electricity ($14 per night), 25 walk-in sites ($10 per night), five group sites (7-25 people, $40), some pull-thrus, picnic tables, drinking water, hot showers, flush toilets, amphitheater, dump station, trails, public phones, 14 day maximum stay.

Minnesota

1 Grand Portage National Monument
2 Voyageurs National Park

Activities Chart

Park												
1		•		•		•				•	•	
2		•		•	•	•	•	•	•	•	•	•

Grand Portage National Monument

PO Box 668
Grand Marais, MN 55604
Phone: 218-387-2788
Fax: 218-387-2790

Grand Portage National Monument is in northeast Minnesota about 35 miles northeast of Grand Marais. Established in 1951, the park preserves a vital headquarters of 18th, 19th, and 20th century fur trade activity and Ojibwe heritage. An entrance fee of $3 is charged for individuals or $6 for families.

Information is available at the monument, which is located at 211 Mile Creek Road in Grand Portage. The monument is open late May to early October. Hours are 9:00 a.m. to 5:00 p.m. Features include the annual Grand Portage Rendezvous Days and Pow-Wow, which occurs the second full weekend of August each year.

Camping is permitted in the monument at Fort Charlotte on the Pigeon River, which is reached by hiking the Grand Portage 8½ miles from the historic stockade or four miles from the crossing at Old Highway 61.

- **Fort Charlotte**: two primitive sites that can accommodate ten people, picnic tables, fire pits, pit toilets, no charge for camping but a backcountry permit is required. Water from the Pigeon River or Snow Creek is not potable; it should be treated before consuming.

Voyageurs National Park

3131 Highway 53 S
International Falls, MN 56649
Phone: 218-283-9821 or 218-286-5258
Fax: 218-285-7407

Voyageurs National Park is located in northern Minnesota 15 miles east of International Falls. Established in 1975, the 218,054-acre park was once the route of the French-Canadian voyageurs. The park remains open year-round. No entrance fee is charged.

Three visitor centers provide information about the park and its history. Ash River Visitor Center is about 40 miles southeast of International Falls via US 53 and CR 129. It is open mid-May through September. Kabetogama Lake Visitor Center is 24 miles southeast of International Falls via US 53 and CR 122. It is also open mid-May through September. Rainy Lake Visitor Center is open year-round. It is located ten miles east of International Falls off MN 11.

There are 210 water accessible campsites throughout the park designed for either tent camping or houseboats. Designated tent sites have a mooring aid, tent pad, fire ring, privy, picnic table, and bear-proof food storage locker. Houseboat sites include two mooring aids and a fire ring. There are no camping fees but a permit is required and is available from the visitor centers. Campsites are available on a first-come, first-served basis. Lodging is available at the historic Kettle Falls Hotel.

Mississippi

1   Gulf Islands National Seashore, *see Florida*
2   Natchez Trace Parkway

Activities Chart

Park

2

Natchez Trace Parkway

2680 Natchez Trace Parkway
Tupelo, MS 38804
Phone: 800-305-7417 or 662-680-4025
Fax: 662-680-4033

Natchez Trace Parkway is a 445-mile route across Mississippi, Alabama, and Tennessee. It generally follows the trace, or trail, used by American Indians and early settlers. The parkway was established in 1938. It is included in the National Scenic Byways Program as an All-American Road. Natchez Trace Parkway is unfinished in Mississippi at the south end and in the Jackson area.

The only visitor center is located in Tupelo at milepost 266. Several remote contact stations are located along the parkway. The center is open from 8:00 a.m. to 5:00 p.m. daily except Christmas Day.

There are three National Park Service campgrounds along Natchez Trace Parkway. Camping is also available in several state parks and in the Tombigbee National Forest near Tupelo.

- **Jeff Busby**: in Mississippi at milepost 193.1 about 12 miles south of Mathiston, open all year, 18 RV/tent sites, no camping fee, concessionaire operated service station and camp store, picnic tables, trail, restrooms, public phone, 14 day maximum stay.

- **Meriwether Lewis**: in Tennessee at milepost 385.9 about seven miles east of Hohenwald, open all year, 32 RV/tent sites, no camping fee, picnic tables, restrooms, nature trails, 14 day maximum stay.

- **Rocky Springs**: in Mississippi at milepost 54.8 about 15 miles northeast of Port Gibson, open all year, 22 RV/tent sites, no camping fee, picnic tables, restrooms, nature trails, public phone, 14 day maximum stay.

Missouri

1   Ozark National Scenic Riverways

Activities Chart

Park											
1	•	•	•	•	•	•	•	•	•	•	•

Ozark National Scenic Riverways

PO Box 490
Van Buren, MO 63965
Phone: 573-323-4236
Fax: 573-323-4140

Ozark National Scenic Riverways consist of 134 miles of the Current and Jacks Fork rivers in southeast Missouri. The area was established in 1972 and encompasses 80,790 acres. No entrance fee is charged.

Although no formal visitor center exists, information can be obtained from park headquarters in Van Buren. The office is located just east of town at 404 Watercress Drive. It is open all year between 8:00 a.m. and 4:30 p.m. Features include exhibits on the resources and history of the Ozarks, informational brochures, and books.

There are five campgrounds available to visitors. All campsites are only available on a first-come, first-served basis.

- **Alley Spring**: located six miles west of Eminence off MO 106, open all year, 187 campsites, $12 per night, 14 day maximum stay, hot showers, flush toilets, dump station, river access.

- **Big Spring**: located four miles south of Van Buren off MO 103, open all year, 131 campsites, $12 per night, 14 day maximum stay, hot showers, flush toilets, dump station, river access.

- **Pulltite**: 24 miles north of Eminence via MO 19 and State Highway EE, open all year, 55 campsites, $12 per night, 14 day maximum stay, flush toilets, river access.

- **Round Spring**: located off MO 19 about 16 miles north of Eminence, open all year, 60 campsites, $12 per night, 14 day maximum stay, hot showers, dump station, flush toilets, river access, cave tours ($5).

- **Two Rivers**: located seven miles east of Eminence via MO 106 and State Highway V, open all year, 12 campsites, $12 per night, flush toilets, showers, 14 day maximum stay, river access.

Montana

1 Bighorn Canyon National Recreation Area
2 Glacier National Park
3 Yellowstone National Park, *see Wyoming*

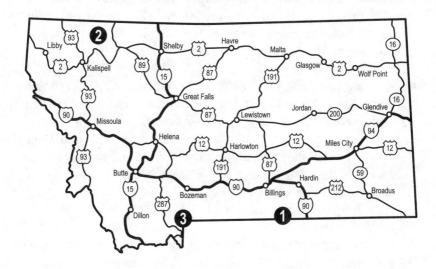

Activities Chart

Park	🚐	🚲	🥾	🐴	🏕	🚤	🛶	🚣	🏊	🎿	⛷
1	•	•	•			•	•		•	•	•
2	•	•	•	•	•	•	•		•	•	•

Bighorn Canyon National Recreation Area

PO Box 7458
Fort Smith, MT 59035
Phone: 406-666-2412 or 307-548-2251
Fax: 406-666-2415

Bighorn Canyon National Recreation Area is in south-central Montana and northern Wyoming. The park was established in 1966 and encompasses 120,296 acres. The north and south ends are not connected by a direct road. Access to the north end is via MT 313 south of Hardin. The south end is accessed from US 14A near Lovell, Wyoming. An entrance fee of $5 is charged.

Information is available from two visitor centers and one ranger station. Yellowtail Dam Visitor Center is in the north end of the park in Fort Smith, Montana. The center is open Memorial Day to Labor Day and has exhibits on the construction and operation of Yellowtail Dam. Bighorn Canyon Visitor Center is in Lovell, Wyoming about ten miles southwest of the southern entrance to the park. It is open all year. Crooked Creek Ranger Station is on WY 37 just beyond the southern entrance. It remains open year-round.

There are five campgrounds in Bighorn Canyon National Recreation Area. Campsites are available on a first-come, first-served basis; no reservations accepted. Black Canyon and Medicine Creek are boat-in campgrounds.

- **Afterbay**: in Montana about 42 miles south of Hardin off MT 313, open all year, 29 RV/tent sites, $5 per night, picnic tables, grills, bear-proof food containers, vault restrooms, boat ramp, drinking water, dump station, 14 day maximum stay.

- **Black Canyon**: boat-in campground located five miles south of Ok-A-Beh Marina at dayboard 5, 17 tent sites, picnic tables, grills, bear-proof food storage, vault toilets.

- **Horseshoe Bend**: in Wyoming about 13 miles north of Lovell off WY 37, open all year, 54 RV/tent sites, $5 per night, picnic tables, grills, flush toilets, boat ramp, drinking water, dump station, 14 day maximum stay.

- **Medicine Creek**: boat-in or hike-in campground north of Barry's Landing at dayboard 32, open year-round, six tent sites, picnic tables, grills, vault toilet, boat docks, no drinking water.

- **Trail Creek**: located along Barry's Landing Road off WY 37, open all year, five tent sites and seven RV sites, $5 per night, 16-foot RV length limit, 14 day maximum stay, picnic tables, grills, bear-proof food storage, vault toilets, boat ramp nearby, no drinking water.

Glacier National Park

Park Headquarters
West Glacier, MT 59936
Phone: 406-888-7800
Fax: 406-888-7808

Glacier National Park is in northwest Montana about 140 miles north of Missoula. The park was established in 1910 and preserves over one million acres of mountains and glaciers. An entrance fee of $10 per vehicle is charged that is valid for seven days.

Visitor centers are located in Apgar, Logan Pass, and Saint Mary. Each of these visitor centers, as well as the Many Glacier and Two Medicine Ranger Stations, have park rangers on duty throughout summer months. During the winter, Apgar Visitor Center is open on weekends. It is located two miles north of West Glacier, the western entrance to the park. Logan Pass Visitor Center is located along the Going-to-the-Sun Road. The Saint Mary Visitor Center is located just west of Saint Mary off US 89.

Glacier National Park has 13 campgrounds. Most campsites are available on a first-come, first-served basis. Fish Creek and Saint Mary Campgrounds have sites that may be reserved up to five months in advance by calling 800-365-2267. Utility hookups are not available in any campground. Backcountry camping is allowed; a permit, available for free, is required. Primitive camping is permitted in many of these campgrounds after the listed dates if road conditions are good.

- **Apgar**: two miles north of West Glacier off Going-to-the-Sun Road, open May to through August, 194 sites, $15 per night, 40-foot RV length limit, flush toilets, dump station, hiker/biker sites available, seven day maximum stay in July and August, 14 day maximum stay rest of year.

- **Avalanche**: on Going-to-the-Sun Road about 14 miles northeast of West Glacier, open mid-June through August, 87 sites, $15 per night, 26-foot RV length limit, flush toilets, dump station, hiker/biker sites available, seven day maximum stay in July and August, 14 day maximum stay rest of year.

- **Bowman Lake**: 30 miles northwest of West Glacier and six miles east of Polebridge via North Fork Road, open mid-May to mid-September, 48 sites, $12 per night, RVs not recommended, primitive campground accessible by dirt road only, seven day maximum stay in July and August, 14 day maximum stay rest of year.

- **Cut Bank**: located ten miles northwest of Kiowa via US 89 and dirt road, open June to late September, 19 sites, $12 per night, pit toilets, RVs not recommended, primitive campground accessible by dirt road only, seven day maximum stay in July and August, 14 day maximum stay rest of year.

- **Fish Creek**: off Camas Creek Road four miles north of West Glacier, open June to mid-October, 180 sites, $17 per night, RV length limit of 35 feet, flush toilets, dump station, reservations accepted (800-365-2267), seven day maximum stay in July and August, 14 day maximum stay rest of year.

- **Kintla Lake**: located about 43 miles north of West Glacier via North Fork Road, open mid May to mid-September, 13 sites, $12 per night, RVs not recommended, primitive campground accessible by dirt road only, seven day maximum stay in July and August, 14 day maximum stay rest of year.

- **Logging Creek**: north of West Glacier along North Fork Road, open July and August, eight sites, $12 per night, RVs not recommended, primitive campground accessible by dirt road only, seven day maximum stay.

- **Many Glacier**: located 12 miles west of Babb on Many Glacier Road, open late May to late September, 110 sites, $15 per night, RV length limit of 35 feet, flush toilets, dump station, hiker/biker sites available, food services, seven day stay limit in July and August, 14 days rest of year.

- **Quartz Creek**: north of West Glacier along North Fork Road, open July and August, seven sites, $12 per night, RVs not recommended, primitive campground accessible by dirt road only, seven day maximum stay.

- **Rising Sun**: six miles west of Saint Mary on Going-to-the-Sun Road, open late May to mid-September, 83 sites, $15 per night, 30-foot RV length limit, flush toilets, showers, dump station, hiker/biker sites available, groceries, seven day maximum stay in July and August, 14 day maximum stay rest of year.

- **Sprague Creek**: on Going-to-the-Sun Road ten miles north of West Glacier, open mid-May to late September, 25 sites, $15 per night, no towed units allowed, flush toilets, seven day maximum stay in July and August, 14 day maximum stay rest of year.

- **Saint Mary**: just west of Saint Mary along Going-to-the-Sun Road, open late May to late September, 148 sites, $17 per night, 35-foot RV length limit, flush toilets, dump station, reservations accepted (800-365-2267), hiker/biker sites available, seven day maximum stay in July and August, 14 day maximum stay rest of year.

- **Two Medicine**: 13 miles northwest of East Glacier Park via MT 49 and Two Medicine Road, open late May to late September, 99 sites, $15 per night, 32-foot RV length limit, flush toilets, dump station, hiker/biker sites available, seven day maximum stay in July and August, 14 day maximum stay rest of year.

Nevada

1   Great Basin National Park
2   Lake Mead National Recreation Area

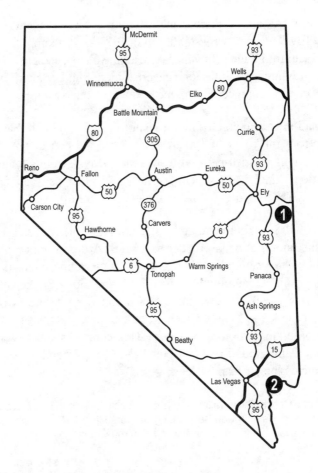

Activities Chart

Park	🚗	🚲	🥾	🐎	⛷️	🛶	🏄	🎿	🏊	❌	🎣	🛥️
1	•	•	•	•	•		•			•	•	
2	•	•	•		•	•	•	•	•	•		

Great Basin National Park

100 Great Basin National Park
Baker, NV 89311
Phone: 775-234-7331
Fax: 775-234-7269

Great Basin National Park is in east-central Nevada about 60 miles east of Ely. The park was established in 1986 and encompasses 77,180 acres. Features include streams, lakes, alpine plants, ancient bristlecone pines, and numerous limestone caverns, including Lehman Caves. No entrance fee is charged. Cave tour fees vary from $2 to $8.

Information is available from the visitor center on NV 488 about five miles from the town of Baker. The center is open all year except Thanksgiving, Christmas, and New Year's Day. Exhibits feature cave formations, ancient bristlecone pines, and other seasonal exhibits. Regularly scheduled tours of Lehman Caves are offered year-round.

Visitors will find four campgrounds within the park. All campsites are available on a first-come, first-served basis. A dump station is located near the visitor center. In addition to the four campgrounds described below, primitive camping areas can be found along Snake Creek and Strawberry Creek Roads. Picnic tables and fire pits are provided at these areas. A few Snake Creek Road campgrounds have pit toilets. Please note the portion of Wheeler Peak Scenic Drive between Upper Lehman Campground and Wheeler Peak Campground is not suitable for vehicles longer than 24 feet.

- **Baker Creek**: three miles south of visitor center on Baker Creek Road, open mid-May through September, 32 campsites, $10 per night, pit toilets, water available in summer only, 14 day maximum stay.

- **Lower Lehman**: two miles from visitor center on Wheeler Peak Scenic Drive, open all year, 11 sites, $10 per night, pit toilets, limited number of pull-through sites, 32-foot RV length limit, water available in summer only, 14 day maximum stay.

- **Upper Lehman**: three miles from visitor center along Wheeler Peak Scenic Drive, open mid-May through September, 24 campsites, $10 per night, pit toilets, water available in summer only, 30-foot RV length limit, 14 day maximum stay.

- **Wheeler Peak**: located 12 miles from visitor center at the end of Wheeler Peak Scenic Drive, open June through September, 37 campsites, $10 per night, 16-foot RV length limit, pit toilets, water available only in summer, 14 day maximum stay. The road to this campground is narrow, curvy, and climbs an eight percent grade. RVs and vehicles pulling trailers are not recommended.

Lake Mead National Recreation Area

601 Nevada Highway
Boulder City, NV 89005
Phone: 702-293-8907 or 702-293-8990
Fax: 702-293-8936

Lake Mead National Recreation Area is in southeast Nevada and northwest Arizona. It was established in 1964 and encompasses nearly 1.5 million acres. Features include Lake Mead, formed by Hoover Dam, and Lake Mohave, formed by Davis Dam on the Colorado River and over one million acres of surrounding desert and mountains. An entrance fee of $5 is charged that is valid for five days.

Information is available from the Alan Bible Visitor Center located east of Boulder City off US 93. The center is open from 8:30 a.m. to 4:30 p.m. every day except Thanksgiving, Christmas, and New Year's Day. Information is also available from various information stations and contact stations.

There are seven National Park Service campgrounds in the recreation area. All campsites are available on a first-come, first-served basis; no reservations accepted. Other concessionaire-operated campgrounds that have sites with hookups are also available. Backcountry camping is permitted.

- **Boulder Beach**: six miles north of Boulder City off NV 166, open all year, 154 RV/tent sites, $10 per night, 30 day stay limit, restrooms, water, dump station, grills, picnic tables.

- **Callville Bay**: 22 miles northeast of Henderson via NV 147 and NV 167, open all year, 80 RV/tent sites, $10 per night, 30 day maximum stay, restrooms, water, dump station, grills, picnic tables.

- **Cottonwood Cove**: on Lake Mohave 14 miles east of Searchlight on NV 164, open all year, 149 RV/tent sites, $10 per night, restrooms, water, dump station, grills, picnic tables, 30 day stay limit in upper campground, 15 day maximum stay in lower campground.

- **Echo Bay**: 30 miles south of Overton via NV 169 and NV 167, open all year, 166 RV/tent sites, $10 per night, 30 day maximum stay, restrooms, water, dump station, grills, picnic tables.

- **Katherine Landing**: in Arizona five miles north of Bullhead City off AZ 68, open all year, 173 RV/tent sites, $10 per night, 30 day maximum stay, restrooms, water, dump station, grills, picnic tables.

- **Las Vegas Bay**: eight miles northeast of Henderson off NV 147, open all year, 89 RV/tent sites, $10 per night, 30 day maximum stay, restrooms, water, dump station, grills, picnic tables.

- **Temple Bar**: in Arizona 80 miles north of Kingman via US 93, open all year, 153 RV/tent sites, $10 per night, 30 day maximum stay, restrooms, water, dump station, grills, picnic tables.

New Mexico

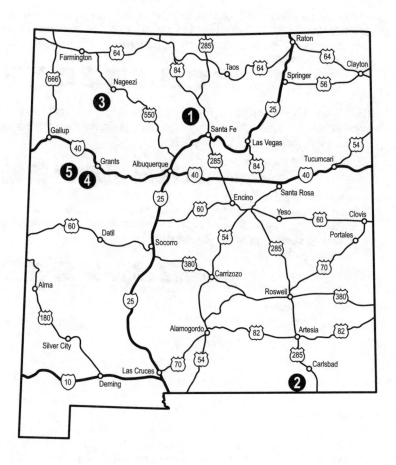

Activities Chart

Park												
1			•						•			
2			•									
3		•	•		•							
4	•	•	•	•	•					•		
5			•							•		

Bandelier National Monument

HCR 1 Box 1 Suite 15
Los Alamos, NM 87544
Phone: 505-672-0343
Fax: 505-672-9607

Bandelier National Monument is in north-central New Mexico about 40 miles west of Santa Fe. Features 13th century Pueblo Indian cliff houses and villages on mesa tops and canyon walls. The 33,676-acre monument was established in 1932. An entrance fee of $10 is charged and is good for seven days.

Information is available from the visitor center located off NM 4 in Frijoles Canyon, three miles from the park entrance. The center is open all year except on Christmas and New Year's Day. Features exhibits on the Pueblo Indian culture. Because of severe space limitations, RVers cannot park in the visitor center's parking lot but must park their RV at Juniper Campground.

There is one campground in the monument. Campsites are available on a first-come, first-served basis; no reservations are accepted. Backcountry camping requires a permit, available for free at the visitor center.

- **Juniper**: located on the mesa top near the park entrance, open March through November, 94 RV/tent sites, $10 per night, picnic tables, fire grills, water, flush toilets, dump station, evening programs offered at amphitheater in summer, 14 day maximum stay, 41-foot RV length limit.

Carlsbad Caverns National Park

3225 National Parks Highway
Carlsbad, NM 88220
Phone: 505-785-2232 or 505-885-8884
Fax: 505-785-2302

Carlsbad Caverns National Park is in southeast New Mexico about 20 miles south of Carlsbad. It was established in 1923 and encompasses 46,766 acres. It was established to preserve Carlsbad Cavern and numerous other caves. The park contains over 85 known caves. An entrance fee of $6 per person is charged that is valid for three days. Fees for cave tours vary from $7 to $20.

Carlsbad Caverns Visitor Center is seven miles from the park entrance near White's City on US 62/180. It is open year-round. Summer hours are 8:00 a.m. to 7:00 p.m. and 8:00 a.m. to 5:00 p.m. the rest of the year. It closes on Christmas Day. The center features exhibits on bats, geology, cave restoration, and park history.

There are no developed campgrounds within the park. Backcountry camping requires a permit that is available for free at the visitor center. Camping is allowed in designated wilderness areas only. Campsites must be at least one-quarter mile away from roads and trails and 300 feet from any natural water source. Campfires are not permitted within the park; use only campstoves. Entering caves without written permission of the superintendent is prohibited.

Chaco Culture National Historical Park

PO Box 220
Nageezi, NM 87037
Phone: 505-786-7014
Fax: 505-786-7061

Chaco Culture National Historical Park is in northwest New Mexico about 70 miles southeast of Farmington. The park encompasses nearly 34,000 acres and was originally established in 1907 as the Chaco Canyon National Monument. The park contains 13 major prehistoric sites and hundreds of smaller ones built by the Ancestral Puebloan People. The entrance fee is $8 per vehicle and is good for seven days.

Information is available from the visitor center located 24 miles south of Nageezi. Getting to the park can be a little difficult. The recommended route from Nageezi is to follow US 550 south three miles to CR 7900 and then CR 7950 and CR 7985. You'll encounter five miles of paved road (CR 7900) and sixteen miles of dirt road. The visitor center is a few miles from the park entrance. The center is open all year and has exhibits on the cultural history of Chaco Canyon.

There is one campground in the park. Campsites are available on a first-come, first-served basis; no reservations are accepted. Gathering of firewood is prohibited; bring in what you may need.

- **Gallo**: located one mile east of the visitor center, 48 sites, $10 per night, picnic tables, fireplaces, centrally located toilets, drinking water available at visitor center, 30-foot RV length limit, seven day maximum stay.

El Malpais National Monument

123 E Roosevelt Ave
Grants, NM 87020
Phone: 505-285-4641 or 505-783-4774
Fax: 505-285-5661

El Malpais National Monument is in west-central New Mexico about 75 miles west of Albuquerque. The park was established in 1987 and encompasses 114,276 acres. El Malpais is a spectacular volcanic area, featuring cinder cones, a 17-mile-long lava tube system, and ice caves. El Malpais is managed by a joint effort between the National Park Service and Bureau of Land Management. No entrance fee is charged.

Information is available from El Malpais Information Center, which is located 23 miles south of Grants on NM 53. The center is open all year from 8:30 a.m. to 4:30 p.m. except on Thanksgiving Day, Christmas Day, and New Year's Day. Rangers conduct a variety of programs, hikes, and demonstrations during summer. Information can also be obtained at the Northwest New Mexico Visitor Center on I-40 at Exit 85.

There are no developed campgrounds within the monument. The Bureau of Land Management allows camping at the Narrows Picnic Area on NM 117. Access by RV in this area is possible but large vehicles should be aware of some tight turns. The National Park Service also allows primitive camping in certain areas. A free backcountry camping permit is required and can be obtained at the information center. Other public campgrounds can be found in nearby Cibola National Forest.

El Morro National Monument

Route 2 Box 43
Ramah, NM 87321
Phone: 505-783-4226
Fax: 505-783-4689

El Morro National Monument is in west-central New Mexico, 43 miles southwest of Grants along NM 53. Established in 1906, the 1,278-acre monument features "Inscription Rock," upon which are carved thousands of inscriptions from early travelers. The monument also includes petroglyphs and Pueblo Indian ruins. An entrance fee of $3 per person is charged and is good for seven days.

Information is available from the visitor center located along the entrance road. The center is open year-round between 9:00 a.m. and 5:00 p.m. except on Christmas Day and New Year's Day. Features include a 15-minute video about the park and a museum.

There is one small campground in the monument. Campsites are available on a first-come, first-served basis. Facilities are limited in winter (water is shut off). There is no fee for camping during winter.

- **El Morro**: located along entrance road off NM 53, open all year, nine sites, $5 per night, picnic tables, drinking water, fire grills, pit toilets, 32-foot RV length limit, 14 day maximum stay, no hookups.

New York

1   Fire Island National Seashore

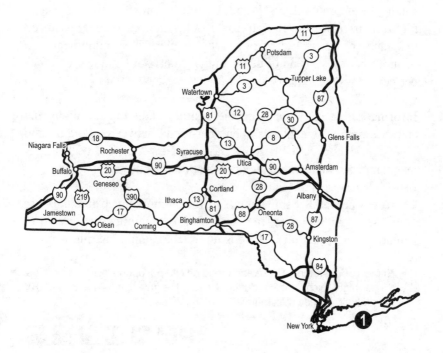

Activities Chart

Park											
1		•			•	•	•	•	•	•	

Fire Island National Seashore

120 Laurel St
Patchogue, NY 11772
Phone: 631-289-4810
Fax: 631-289-4898

Fire Island National Seashore is in southeast New York about 60 miles east of New York City. Established in 1964, the 19,578-acre park features beaches, dunes, Fire Island Light, and the nearby estate of William Floyd, a signer of the Declaration of Independence. No entrance fee is charged.

There are no public roads on the island itself; getting around requires walking or using water taxis. Access to the island is via Robert Moses Causeway on the western end or William Floyd Parkway on the eastern end. There are parking lots for visitors to the national seashore.

Information is available from four visitor centers. Fire Island Lighthouse Visitor Center is at the western end, adjacent to Robert Moses State Park. Sailors Haven is in the middle of Fire Island, across the Great South Bay from Sayville, Long Island. The center is reached by ferry and is closed in winter. The Watch Hill Visitor Center is also accessed by ferry from Patchogue and is only open in summer. At the east end of Fire Island is the Wilderness Visitor Center, accessible by car via William Floyd Parkway. The center is open from April through December.

The park's only campground is near Watch Hill Visitor Center. Campsite reservations are strongly recommended. Visitors without reservations may be able to obtain a site depending on availability. For reservation information call 631-289-9336.

- **Watch Hill**: open mid-May to mid-October, 26 tent sites, $15 per night, water, grills, showers, bathrooms. A marina, snack bar, restaurant, and life guarded beach are nearby.

North Carolina

1   Blue Ridge Parkway
2   Cape Hatteras National Seashore
3   Cape Lookout National Seashore
4   Great Smoky Mountains National Park, *see Tennessee*

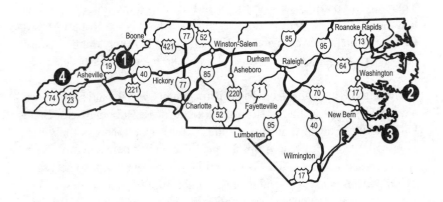

Activities Chart

Park	🚗	🚲	🥾	🐎	🤸	🛶	⛵	🏄	🏊	✈	🎿	🛷
1	•	•	•	•	•	•	•			•	•	
2	•	•	•		•	•	•	•	•	•		
3					•	•	•	•	•			

Blue Ridge Parkway

199 Hemphill Knob Rd
Asheville, NC 28803
Phone: 828-298-0398
Fax: 828-271-4313

Blue Ridge Parkway runs 469 miles between Shenandoah National Park in Virginia and Great Smoky Mountains National Park in North Carolina. The parkway was established in 1936 and encompasses 88,734 acres. It is included in the National Scenic Byways Program as an All-American Road. No entrance fee is charged.

The parkway is marked every mile by concrete mileposts beginning at MP 0 near Shenandoah National Park and ending at MP 469 at Great Smoky Mountains National Park. Knowing this will help in locating visitor centers and campgrounds.

There are 12 visitor centers along the parkway. All are generally open from May through October. Visitor centers can be found at the following mileposts: Humpback Rocks, MP 5.8; James River, MP 63.8; Peaks of Otter, MP 86.0; Virginia's Explore Park, MP 115; Rocky Knob, MP 169.0; Cumberland Knob, MP 217.5; Northwest Trading Post, MP 258.6; Moses H. Cone Memorial Park, MP 294.1; Linn Cove Viaduct, MP 305; Linville Falls, MP 316.4; Craggy Gardens, MP 364.6; Waterrock Knob, MP 451.2.

There are nine campgrounds along the parkway. They are listed in milepost order; the first listed is near the beginning of the parkway in Virginia. All campsites are available on a first-come, first-served basis; reservations are not accepted. Limited backcountry camping is available at Basin Cove in Doughton Park and Rock Castle Gorge in Rocky Knob District. Permits are required and must be requested in advance.

- **Otter Creek**: at MP 60.9, open May through September, 45 tent sites, 24 RV sites, $14 per night, drinking water, restrooms, picnic tables, fireplace, dump station, telephone, self-guiding trail, fishing, 21 day maximum stay in summer, 30-foot RV length limit.

- **Peaks of Otter**: at MP 86.0, open May through October, 82 tent sites, 59 RV sites, $14 per night, drinking water, restrooms, picnic tables, fireplace, dump station, camping supplies, telephone, self-guiding trails, fishing, 21 day maximum stay in summer, 30-foot RV length limit.

- **Roanoke Mountain**: at MP 120.5, open May through October, 74 tent sites, 30 RV sites, $14 per night, drinking water, restrooms, picnic tables, fireplace, dump station, telephone, 21 day stay limit in summer, 30-foot RV length limit.

- **Rocky Knob**: at MP 167.1, open May through October, 81 tent sites, 28 RV sites, $14 per night, drinking water, restrooms, picnic tables, fireplace, dump station, telephone, nature trails, fishing, 21 day maximum stay in summer, 30-foot RV length limit.

- **Doughton Park**: at MP 239.0, open May through October, 110 tent sites, 25 RV sites, $14 per night, drinking water, restrooms, picnic tables, fireplace, dump station, camping supplies, telephone, fishing, 21 day maximum stay in summer, 30-foot RV length limit.

- **Julian Price Memorial Park**: at MP 297.1, open May through October, 129 tent sites, 68 RV sites, $14 per night, drinking water, restrooms, picnic tables, fireplace, dump station, telephone, fishing, 21 day maximum stay in summer, 30-foot RV length limit.

- **Linville Falls**: at MP 316.3, open May through October, 50 tent sites, 20 RV sites, $14 per night, drinking water, restrooms, picnic tables, fireplace, dump station, nature trails, fishing, 21 day stay limit in summer, 30-foot RV length limit.

- **Crabtree Meadows**: at MP 339.5, open May through October, 71 tent sites, 22 RV sites, $14 per night, drinking water, restrooms, picnic tables, fireplace, dump station, camping supplies, telephone, 21 day maximum stay in summer, 30-foot RV length limit.

- **Mount Pisgah**: at MP 408.6, open May through October, 70 tent sites, 67 RV sites, $14 per night, drinking water, restrooms, picnic tables, fireplace, dump station, camping supplies, telephone, 21 day maximum stay in summer, 30-foot RV length limit.

Cape Hatteras National Seashore

1401 National Park Dr
Manteo, NC 27954
Phone: 252-473-2111 or 252-441-5711
Fax: 252-473-2595

Cape Hatteras National Seashore is in eastern North Carolina. It was established in 1953 and encompasses 30,319 acres. Features include sandy beaches, migratory waterfowl, fishing, and historical points of interest. No entrance fee is charged.

Information is available from three visitor centers. Bodie Island Visitor Center is about seven miles south of Whalebone Junction off NC 12. The center is open year-round. Hatteras Island Visitor Center is near Buxton off NC 12 in the Cape Hatteras Lighthouse. It is open all year. Ocracoke Visitor Center is off NC 12 in Ocracoke. It remains open year-round. All visitor centers close on Christmas Day.

There are four campgrounds in the park. Reservations can be made for campsites in Ocracoke Campground from May and mid-September by calling 800-365-2267. Campsites in all other campgrounds are available on a first-come, first-served basis.

- **Cape Point**: two miles south of Buxton off NC 12 near Cape Hatteras Lighthouse, open Memorial Day to Labor Day, 202 sites, $18 per night, drinking water, cold showers, flush toilets, picnic tables, grills, dump station nearby, 14 day maximum stay.

- **Frisco**: off NC 12 east of Frisco and southwest of Buxton, open mid-April to mid-October, 127 sites, $18 per night, cold showers, flush toilets, drinking water, picnic tables, grills, 14 day maximum stay.

- **Ocracoke**: east of Ocracoke along NC 12, open mid-April to mid-October, 136 RV/tent sites, $18 per night, cold showers, flush toilets, drinking water, picnic tables, grills, dump station nearby, 14 day maximum stay.

- **Oregon Inlet**: nine miles south of Whalebone Junction along NC 12, open mid-April to mid-October, 120 sites, $18 per night, cold showers, flush toilets, drinking water, picnic tables, grills, dump station nearby, marina nearby, 14 day maximum stay.

Cape Lookout National Seashore

131 Charles St
Harkers Island, NC 28531
Phone: 252-728-2250
Fax: 252-728-2160

Cape Lookout National Seashore is in eastern North Carolina. The seashore is a 56-mile section of the Outer Banks of North Carolina between Ocracoke Inlet and Beaufort Inlet. It was established in 1966. No entrance fee is charged. Access to the area is by ferry; cost varies.

Information is available from the visitor center on Harkers Island, which is open daily from 8:00 a.m. to 4:30 p.m. It is closed on December 25 and January 1. Visitor centers in the Lighthouse Keepers Quarters and in Portsmouth Village are open from April to November; hours vary.

There are no designated campgrounds in the park but primitive camping is allowed. There is very little shade or shelter on the islands and no source for supplies. Campers must bring everything they need, including drinking water. Campers must pack out all trash. Camping is limited to 14 consecutive days. Driftwood campfires are permitted below the high tide line; a permit is not required. It is recommend that visitors bring a campstove. Contact the National Seashore for details about camping.

North Dakota

1　Theodore Roosevelt National Park

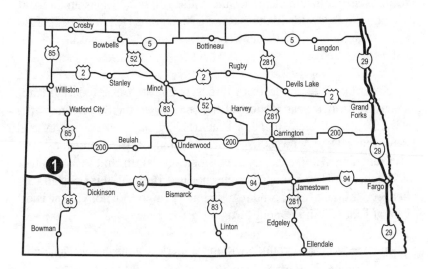

Activities Chart

Park											
1	•	•	•	•	•	•	•	•	•		•	•

Theodore Roosevelt National Park

PO Box 7
Medora, ND 58645
Phone: 701-623-4466 or 701-842-2333
Fax: 701-623-4840

Theodore Roosevelt National Park is in southwest North Dakota about 135 miles west of Bismarck. Established in 1947, the 70,446-acre park features scenic badlands along the Little Missouri River and part of Theodore Roosevelt's Elkhorn Ranch. An entrance fee of $5 per person with a maximum of $10 per vehicle is charged. The entrance fee is valid for seven days.

Information is available from three visitor centers. Medora Visitor Center is located near Medora at the entrance to the South Unit off I-94. It is open all year except on Thanksgiving Day, Christmas Day, and New Year's Day. A museum features exhibits of Theodore Roosevelt, area ranching history, and natural history. The North Unit Visitor Center is just west of US 85 about 54 miles north of Belfield. It is open all year between 9:00 a.m. and 5:30 p.m. Painted Canyon Visitor Center is off I-94 at Exit #32 in the South Unit.

There are two campgrounds within the park. Campsites are available on a first-come, first-served basis; reservations are not accepted.

- **Cottonwood**: located in the South Unit of the park north of Medora, open all year, 59 RV/tent sites, 11 walk-in sites, $10 per night, some pull-thrus, picnic tables, fire grills, flush toilets, drinking water, amphitheater, 14 day maximum stay. Facilities are limited during winter.

- **Juniper**: located in the North Unit of the park six miles from park entrance, open all year, 50 RV/tent sites, $10 per night May through September, $5 per night October through April, some pull-thrus, picnic tables, fire grills, flush toilets, drinking water, dump station, 14 day maximum stay. Facilities are limited during winter.

Oklahoma

1   Chickasaw National Recreation Area

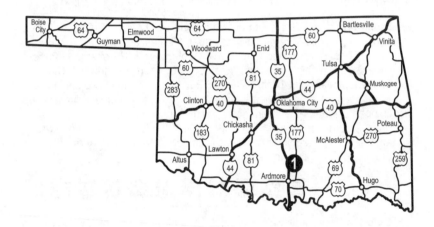

Activities Chart

Park
1   •   •   •   •   •   •   •

Chickasaw National Recreation Area

1008 W Second St
Sulphur, OK 73086
Phone: 580-622-3161 or 580-622-3165
Fax: 580-622-2296

Chickasaw National Recreation Area is in south-central Oklahoma about 80 miles south of Oklahoma City. The recreation area was originally established as Sulphur Springs Reservation in 1906 and later renamed and re-designated in 1976. The park encompasses 9,888 acres of springs, streams, and lakes. No entrance fee is charged.

Information is available from the park headquarters in Sulphur off US 177 and from the Travertine Information and Nature Center. The latter is open all year except for Christmas Day and New Year's Day. Daily activities are scheduled throughout the summer including nature walks and campfire programs.

There are five campgrounds within the park. All campsites are available on a first-come, first-served basis; no reservations are accepted.

- **Buckhorn**: nine miles south of Sulphur via US 177 and Buckhorn Road. Loop A: open mid-May to mid-September, 19 sites, $8 per night, restrooms, water. Loop B: open mid-May to mid-September, 6 RV sites and 20 tent sites, $8 per night, restrooms, water. Loop C: open April through October, 27 RV/tent sites and 14 tent sites, $8 per night, 17 sites have electric and water hookups ($14 per night), restrooms, water, amphitheater, trails. Loop D: open all year, 37 RV/tent sites and 12 tent sites, $8 per night, 24 sites have electric and water hookups ($14 per night), restrooms, water, amphitheater. Camping in all loops is limited to 14 days. Boat ramp, picnic area, and dump station nearby.

- **Cold Springs**: near Sulphur about one-half mile east of US 177, open mid-May to early October, 63 tent-only sites, $8 per night, restrooms, water, access to hiking trail, 14 day maximum stay.

- **Guy Sandy**: nine miles southwest of Sulphur via OK 7 and Chickasaw Trail Road, open late May through August, 40 campsites, $8 per night, restrooms, water, 14 day maximum stay. Boat ramp and picnic area nearby.

- **Rock Creek**: just southwest of Sulphur via 12th Street and Lindsay Avenue, open all year, 105 campsites, $8 per night, most tent-only sites but some accommodate RVs, restrooms, water, 14 day maximum stay. Access to hiking trail nearby. Only 38 campsites are open year-round, the rest are open seasonally.

- **The Point**: eight miles southwest of Sulphur via OK 7 and Charles Cooper Memorial Road, open late May through August, 55 sites in two loops, $8 per night, 22 sites have electric and water hookups ($14 per night), restrooms, drinking water, 14 day maximum stay. Loop B is open all year.

Oregon

1   Crater Lake National Park

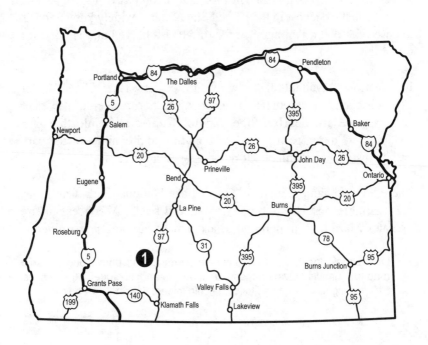

Activities Chart

Park												
1	•	•	•		•		•			•	•	

Crater Lake National Park

PO Box 7
Crater Lake, OR 97604
Phone: 541-594-3100
Fax: 541-594-3010

Crater Lake National Park is in southwest Oregon about 75 miles north of Medford. It was established in 1902 and encompasses 183,244 acres. The lake is the deepest in the United States and is widely known for its intense blue color. An entrance fee of $10 is charged and is good for seven days.

Information is available from two visitor centers. Rim Village Visitor Center is open June through September. A gift shop, cafeteria, and Crater Lake Lodge are nearby. Steel Visitor Center is inside the park headquarters along Rim Drive. A short film and exhibits of the park and its history are available. It remains open all year.

There are two campgrounds in Crater Lake National Park. Campsites are available on a first-come, first-served basis. A concessionaire operates Mazama Campground. Backcountry camping is permitted.

- **Lost Creek**: located in the southeast corner of the park along the spur road to Pinnacles Overlook, open mid-July to early October, 16 tent sites, $10 per night, water, flush toilets, picnic tables, fire rings, 14 day stay.

- **Mazama**: north of OR 62 about 55 miles northwest of Klamath Falls, open mid-June to early October, 96 RV sites ($16 per night), 102 tent sites ($15 per night), water, flush toilets, dump station, picnic tables, fire rings, hot showers, groceries, laundry facilities, 14 day maximum stay.

Pennsylvania

1   Delaware Water Gap National Recreation Area

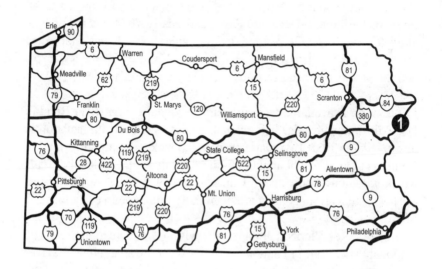

Activities Chart

Park												
1	•	•	•	•	•	•	•	•	•	•	•	•

Delaware Water Gap National Recreation Area

1 River Road
Bushkill, PA 18324
Phone: 570-588-2435 or 570-588-2452
Fax: 570-588-2780

Delaware Water Gap National Recreation Area is in northeast Pennsylvania about 50 miles east of Scranton. The park preserves 40 miles of the middle Delaware River and nearly 70,000 acres of land along the river's New Jersey and Pennsylvania shores. It was established in 1965. In 1978, the river was designated a National Scenic River. No entrance fee is charged but some areas charge a user fee.

Information is available from the park headquarters on River Road in Bushkill, Pennsylvania. It is open weekdays all year. Information is also available from two visitor centers. Bushkill Visitor Information Center is along US 209 about one-quarter mile south of Bushkill Falls Road. Kittatinny Point Visitor Center is in Columbia, New Jersey just off I-80 Exit 1. Both centers are open daily mid-June to early fall.

There are no developed campgrounds within the recreation area. The National Park Service maintains primitive camping areas along the river for boaters traveling from one access point to another. Length of stay is limited to one night. Campsites are available on a first-come, first-served basis. No permit is required and no camping fee is charged. Public and private campgrounds can be found in the surrounding area.

South Carolina

1 Congaree Swamp National Monument
2 Kings Mountain National Military Park

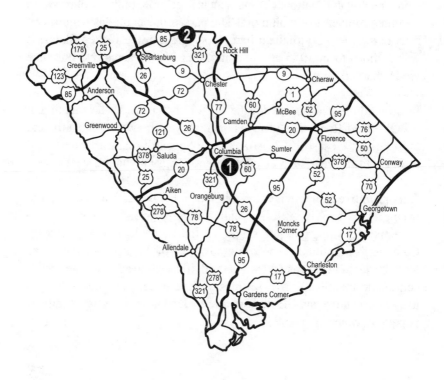

Activities Chart

Park	🚗	🚲	🥾	🐴	🚶	🛶	🦆	🛶	🏊	✈	🏄	⛴
1			•		•	•	•	•		•		
2		•	•									

Congaree Swamp National Monument

100 National Park Road
Hopkins, SC 29061
Phone: 803-776-4396
Fax: 803-783-4241

Congaree Swamp National Monument is in central South Carolina about 20 miles southeast of Columbia. The park protects the last significant tract of southern bottomland hardwood forest in the United States. It was authorized in 1976 and encompasses 21,867 acres. No entrance fee is charged.

Information is available from the visitor center inside the monument off Old Bluff Road. The office is open all year between 8:30 a.m. and 5:00 p.m. It closes on Christmas Day. Special programs are offered throughout the year such as guided canoe trips and nature walks.

Only primitive camping is offered in the park. Over 20 miles of marked hiking trails and 18 miles of marked canoe trails exist within the monument. Camping requires a permit that is available free of charge. Camping is permitted in the wilderness area of the park 100 feet away from backcountry trails and water, and 500 feet away from the visitor center and boardwalk. No facilities are available. Camping is limited to 14 consecutive days. Restrooms are located near the visitor center as is potable water.

Kings Mountain National Military Park

2625 Park Road
Blacksburg, SC 29702
Phone: 864-936-7921
Fax: 864-936-9897

Kings Mountain National Military Park is in north-central South Carolina about 32 miles northwest of Rock Hill. American frontiersmen defeated the British here on October 7, 1780 at a critical point during the Revolution. The park was established in 1933 and encompasses 3,945 acres. No entrance fee is charged.

Information is available from the visitor center located inside the park along Park Road. The center is open daily 9:00 a.m. to 5:00 p.m. and from 9:00 a.m. to 6:00 p.m. weekends between Memorial Day and Labor Day. It is closed Thanksgiving Day, Christmas Day, and New Year's Day. Features include an 18-minute film and museum exhibit area.

There is one designated backcountry campsite within Kings Mountain National Military Park. The campsite is a three-mile hike from the visitor center and holds up to ten people. No advanced registration is required; you can register the day you will be camping. Kings Mountain State Park is adjacent to the military park and has 116 sites with hookups for about $16 per night.

South Dakota

1   Badlands National Park
2   Wind Cave National Park

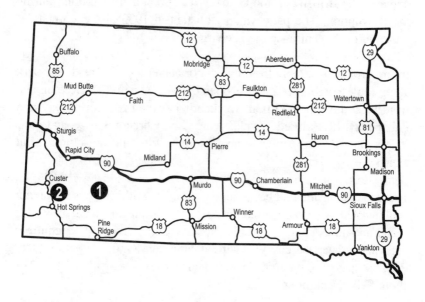

Activities Chart

Park	🚙	🚲	🚶	🐴	🚶	🌊	🛶	🏄	🏊	✈	🏂	🛷
1	•	•	•	•	•					•	•	
2	•	•	•	•	•				•			

Badlands National Park

PO Box 6
Interior, SD 57750
Phone: 605-433-5361
Fax: 605-433-5248

Badlands National Park is in southwest South Dakota about 80 miles east of Rapid City. The park was established in 1929 and consists of 242,755 acres. An entrance fee of $10 is charged that is valid for seven days.

Information is available from the Ben Reifel Visitor Center located eight miles south of I-90 Exit 131. The center is open all year and features exhibits of fossils, cultural history, and prairie ecology. Summer hours are 7:00 a.m. to 7:00 p.m. Information is also available during summer at the White River Visitor Center on Highway 27 in the Pine Ridge Indian Reservation.

There are two National Park Service campgrounds within the park. Campsites are available on a first-come, first-served basis. Lodging is also available at Cedar Pass Lodge, which is open mid-April through mid-October. A restaurant is available at the lodge.

- **Cedar Pass**: near the visitor center off SD 240, open all year, 96 RV/tent sites, $10 per night in summer, $8 per night in winter, limited facilities in winter, flush toilets, dump station, 14 day stay limit, no campfires allowed.

- **Sage Creek**: primitive campground 30 miles northwest of visitor center via SD 240 and Sage Creek Rim Road, open all year, 15 sites, no camping fee, pit toilets, no water, no campfires allowed. Horseback riders frequently use the campground. A high-clearance vehicle is required to travel Sage Creek Rim Road.

Wind Cave National Park

RR 1 Box 190
Hot Springs, SD 57747
Phone: 605-745-4600
Fax: 605-745-4207

Wind Cave National Park is in southwest South Dakota about 50 miles south of Rapid City. The park was established in 1903 and features one of the world's longest and most complex caves and 28,295 acres of mixed-grass prairie and ponderosa pine forest. No entrance fee is charged but fees are charged for cave tours ($6 to $20).

Information is available from the Wind Cave Visitor Center located off US 385 about ten miles north of Hot Springs. The center is open all year except on Thanksgiving Day, Christmas Day, and New Year's Day. All cave tours depart from the visitor center. Exhibits feature cave exploration, formations, and history.

There is one developed campground in the park. Campsites are available on a first-come, first-served basis; no reservations are accepted. Backcountry camping is allowed; a permit is required and is available for free.

- **Elk Mountain:** ten miles north of Hot Springs off US 385, open April through October, 90 RV/tent sites, 25 pull-thrus, $12 per night from mid-May to mid-September, $6 per night otherwise, limited off-season facilities, flush toilets, drinking water, amphitheater, picnic tables, fire grates, nature trail, 14 day maximum stay, 35-foot RV length limit.

Tennessee

1   Big South Fork National River & Recreation Area
2   Cumberland Gap National Historical Park, *see Kentucky*
3   Great Smoky Mountains National Park
4   Natchez Trace Parkway, *see Mississippi*
5   Obed Wild & Scenic River

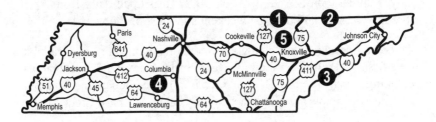

Activities Chart

Park												
1		•	•	•	•	•	•	•	•	•	•	
3	•	•	•	•	•		•			•		
5		•			•	•	•	•	•	•		

Big South Fork National River & Rec. Area

4564 Leatherwood Rd
Oneida, TN 37841
Phone: 423-569-9778 or 423-286-7275
Fax: 423-569-5505

Big South Fork National River and Recreation Area is in northeast Tennessee and southern Kentucky. The park was established in 1974 and encompasses 125,242 acres. It preserves 90 miles of the Big South Fork of the Cumberland River. No entrance fee is charged.

Information is available from two visitor centers. Bandy Creek Visitor Center is 15 miles west of Oneida, Tennessee off TN 297. It is open all year except on Christmas. Stearns Visitor Center is south of Whitley City, Kentucky on KY 92, west of US 27. It is open daily from April through October and only on weekends the rest of the year.

Three campgrounds are available to visitors. Campsites are available on a first-come, first-served basis for sites in Alum Ford. Backcountry camping is permitted. A $5 to $25 fee is collected depending on group size. Also available are rustic backcountry cabins at Charit Creek Lodge.

- **Alum Ford**: in Kentucky 16 miles northwest of Whitley City via US 27 and KY 700, open all year, eight primitive campsites, $5 per night, pit toilets, no drinking water, canoe and boat launch nearby, access to hiking trail, 14 day maximum stay.

- **Bandy Creek**: 15 miles west of Oneida off TN 297 near visitor center, open all year, 100 sites with water and electric hookups ($20 per night), 50 tent sites ($17 per night), restrooms, showers, dump station, swimming pool, reservations accepted from April through October (800-365-2267), 14 day maximum stay.

- **Blue Heron**: located on KY 742 west of Stearns in Kentucky, open April to mid-November, 45 sites with water and electric hookups, $15 per night, restrooms, showers, dump station, reservations accepted (800-365-2267), 14 day maximum stay.

Great Smoky Mountains National Park

107 Park Headquarters Rd
Gatlinburg, TN 37738
Phone: 865-436-1200
Fax: 865-436-1220

Great Smoky Mountains National Park is in eastern Tennessee and western North Carolina. The park was established in 1934 and encompasses 521,621 acres. No entrance fee is charged.

Information is available from three visitor centers. Cades Cove Visitor Center is near the midpoint of Cades Cove Loop Road. It is open year-round and features a variety of exhibits. Oconaluftee Visitor Center is two miles north of Cherokee, North Carolina on US 441. It is open all year. A museum is adjacent to the center. Sugarlands Visitor Center is two miles south of Gatlinburg, Tennessee on US 441. It is open all year and features a 20-minute film and natural history exhibits.

There are ten campgrounds within Great Smoky Mountains National Park. Backcountry camping is allowed in designated sites but a permit, available free, is required. Lodging is available at Le Conte Lodge, which is reached only by a hiking trail. Reservations are required and often must be made one year in advance. Call 865-429-5704 for more information.

- **Abrams Creek**: in Tennessee six miles north of Chilhowee off US 129, open mid-March through October, 16 sites, $12 per night, RV length limit of 12 feet, picnic tables, fire rings, restrooms, running water, seven day maximum stay (5/15 to 10/31), 14 day maximum stay rest of year.

- **Balsam Mountain**: in North Carolina on Balsam Mountain Road northeast of Cherokee via US 19 and Blue Ridge Parkway, open mid-May to mid-October, 46 sites, $14 per night, 30-foot RV length limit, picnic tables, fire rings, restrooms, running water, seven day maximum stay.

- **Big Creek**: in North Carolina near Waterville south of I-40 Exit #451, open mid-March through October, 12 tent sites, $12 per night, picnic tables, fire rings, restrooms, running water, seven day maximum stay.

- **Cades Cove**: in Tennessee on Cades Cove Road, open year-round, 159 sites, $17 per night from mid-May through October, $14 per night off season, 40-foot RV length limit, reservations accepted mid-May through October (800-365-2267), picnic tables, fire rings, restrooms, running water, campstore, dump station, seven day maximum stay (5/15 to 10/31), 14 day maximum stay rest of year.

- **Cataloochee**: in North Carolina near Nellie about ten miles west of I-40 Exit #20 via US 276 and NC 1395, open mid-March through October, 27 sites, $12 per night, 31-foot RV length limit, picnic tables, fire rings, restrooms, running water, seven day maximum stay (5/15 to 10/31), 14 day maximum stay rest of year.

- **Cosby**: in Tennessee two miles south of Cosby off US 321, open mid-March through October, 157 sites, $14 per night, RV length limit of 25 feet, picnic tables, fire rings, restrooms, running water, dump station, seven day maximum stay (5/15 to 10/31), 14 day maximum stay rest of year.

- **Deep Creek**: in North Carolina three miles north of Bryson City via Deep Creek Road, open early April through October, 92 sites, $14 per night, 26-foot RV length limit, picnic tables, fire rings, restrooms, dump station, running water, seven day stay limit (5/15 to 10/31), 14 days rest of year.

- **Elkmont**: in Tennessee eight miles southwest of Gatlinburg via Little River Road, open mid-March through November, 220 sites, $14 per night off season, $17 per night mid-May through October, riverside sites are $20 per night, 32-foot RV length limit, reservations accepted mid-May through October (800-365-2267), picnic tables, fire rings, restrooms, running water, seven day maximum stay (5/15 to 10/31), 14 days rest of year.

• **Look Rock**: in Tennessee off Foothills Parkway between Walland and Chilhowee, open mid-May through October, 92 sites, $14 per night, 35-foot RV length limit, picnic tables, fire rings, restrooms, running water, seven day maximum stay.

• **Smokemont**: in North Carolina six miles north of Cherokee via Newfound Gap Road, open year-round, 140 sites, $17 per night from mid-May through October, $14 per night rest of year, 27-foot RV length limit, reservations accepted from mid-May through October (800-365-2267), picnic tables, fire rings, restrooms, running water, dump station.

Obed Wild & Scenic River

PO Box 429
Wartburg, TN 37887
Phone: 423-346-6294
Fax: 423-346-3362

Obed Wild and Scenic River is in eastern Tennessee about 50 miles west of Knoxville. It includes parts of the Obed River, Clear Creek, Daddy's Creek, and Emory River. Over 45 miles of creeks and rivers are included in the wild and scenic river area. It was established in 1976. There is no entrance fee.

Visitor information is available from the visitor center in Wartburg at 208 North Maiden Street. The center is open all year between 8:00 a.m. and 4:30 p.m. It closes on Christmas Day. Saturday evening interpretive programs are offered on a regular basis during summer. Features include a small exhibit and book sales area.

There is one primitive campground. Camping is also available in the nearby Frozen Head State Park, which has 19 RV/tent campsites for about $13 per night.

- **Rock Creek**: about five miles southwest of Wartburg via Catoosa Road, 12 tent sites, no water or electricity, $7 per night, pit toilets, picnic tables, fire rings. Campsites are available on a first-come, first-served basis.

Texas

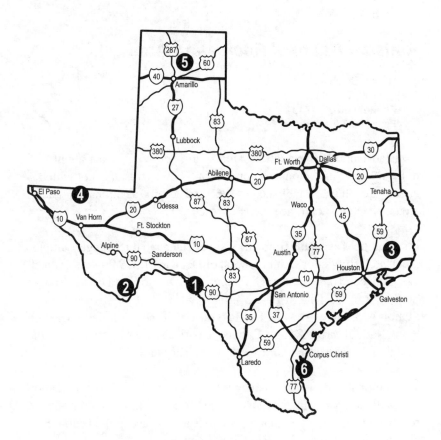

Activities Chart

Park											
1		•	•	•	•	•	•	•	•	•	•
2	•	•	•	•	•		•	•		•	
3	•	•	•	•	•	•	•	•	•	•	
4			•	•	•					•	
5		•	•		•	•			•	•	
6	•	•	•	•	•	•	•	•	•	•	

Amistad National Recreation Area

HCR 3 Box 5J
Del Rio, TX 78840
Phone: 830-775-7491
Fax: 830-775-7299

Amistad National Recreation Area is in southwest Texas about 175 miles west of San Antonio. It consists of 57,292 acres, most of which is under water. It was established in 1965 and became a national recreation area in 1990. No entrance fee is charged.

Information is available from one visitor center and three ranger stations. Amistad Dam Visitor Center is west of Del Rio off US 90. It is open all year between 10:00 a.m. and 6:00 p.m. The Diablo East District Ranger Station is in the Diablo East Marina off US 90. Pecos River Ranger Station is 35 miles west of Del Rio on US 90 near Seminole Canyon State Natural Area. Rough Canyon District Ranger Station is in the Rough Canyon Marina northwest of Del Rio via US 277.

The National Park Service manages four campgrounds in the recreation area. All campsites are available on a first-come, first-served basis; no reservations are accepted. Dump stations are located at the Diablo East entrance road and the Del Rio Civic Center.

- **277 North**: off US 277 about ten miles north of Del Rio, open in summer, 17 sites, $4 per night, picnic tables, grills, vault toilets, no drinking water, no RV length limit, 14 day maximum stay.

- **Governors Landing**: off US 90 about 12 miles west of Del Rio, open all year, 15 sites, $8 per night, picnic tables, grills, vault toilets, drinking water, 28-foot RV length limit, 14 day maximum stay.

- **San Pedro**: off US 90 about seven miles west of Del Rio, open all year, 35 sites, 5 tent-only sites, $4 per night, picnic tables, grills, vault toilets, no drinking water, boat ramp nearby, no RV length limit, 14 day stay limit.

- **Spur 406**: about 28 miles northwest of Del Rio via US 90 and TX 406, open all year, eight sites, $4 per night, picnic tables, grills, vault toilets, no drinking water, no RV length limit, 14 day maximum stay.

Big Bend National Park

PO Box 129
Big Bend National Park, TX 79834
Phone: 432-477-2251
Fax: 432-477-1175

Big Bend National Park is in west Texas about 40 miles south of
Marathon. The 801,163-acre park was established in 1944. Features
include mountains, desert, and deep canyons carved by the Rio Grande
River. An entrance fee of $15 is charged that is valid for seven days.

Information is available from four visitor centers. Chisos Basin Visitor
Center is open all year from 9:00 a.m. to 4:30 p.m. It is located six
miles south of Basin Junction. The road is not recommended for RVs
over 24 feet because of sharp curves and steep grades. Persimmon Gap
Visitor Center is located at the northern entrance off US 385. Panther
Junction Visitor Center is 26 miles from the north entrance and is open
daily from 8:00 a.m. to 6:00 p.m. Rio Grande Village Visitor Center is
about 20 miles southeast of the Panther Junction Visitor Center and is
closed in summer.

There are four campgrounds within Big Bend National Park. Campsites
are available on a first-come, first-served basis. Primitive camping is
available in over 70 campsites that line the park's dirt roads. Backpackers
have access to 42 designated backcountry campsites. A free backcounty
permit is required.

- **Chisos Basin**: six miles south of Basin Junction, open all year, 65
  campsites, $10 per night, flush toilets, dump station, running water, grills,
  picnic tables, nature and hiking trails, 14 day maximum stay. Due to the
  narrow and winding road to Chisos Basin, trailers over 20 feet and RVs
  over 24 feet are not recommended. A lodge and grocery store are nearby.

- **Cottonwood**: 22 miles south of Santa Elena Junction off Ross Maxwell
  Scenic Drive, open all year, 35 campsites, $10 per night, pit toilets, picnic
  tables, grills, drinking water, 14 day maximum stay, 24-foot RV length limit,

groceries nearby. The use of generators is not allowed.

- **Rio Grande Village**: about 20 miles southeast of Panther Junction, open all year, 100 campsites, some pull-thrus, $10 per night, flush toilets, dump station, running water, picnic tables, grills, 14 day maximum stay.

- **Rio Grande Village RV Park**: concession-operated near the National Park Service's Rio Grande Village campground, open all year, 25 RV sites with complete hookups, $18 per night, restrooms, showers, picnic tables, laundry facilities, 14 day maximum stay. Full hookup capability is required.

Big Thicket National Preserve

3785 Milam St
Beaumont, TX 77701
Phone: 409-246-2337 or 409-839-2689
Fax: 409-839-2599

Big Thicket National Preserve is in eastern Texas. It consists of nine land units and six water corridors encompassing more than 97,000 acres. It was established in 1974 to preserve the rich biological diversity of the area. No entrance fee is charged.

Information may be obtained from park headquarters in Beaumont on Milam Street. The headquarters is open Monday through Friday from 8:00 a.m. to 4:30 p.m. Information is also available from Big Thicket Visitor Center, which is open all year except Christmas Day and New Year's Day. The visitor center is 25 miles north of Beaumont via US 69 and FM 420.

There are no developed campgrounds within the park. Visitors come to the preserve to experience backcountry camping. A free permit is required and is available from the park headquarters or visitor center. The permit is valid for ten days. Contact the preserve to obtain a map showing the different units and hiking trails. Several state parks are in the area with developed camping facilities. A Corps of Engineers project, Steinhagen Lake, is east of Woodville along US 190. Developed camping facilities are available there.

Guadalupe Mountains National Park

HC 60 Box 400
Salt Flat, TX 79847
Phone: 915-828-3251
Fax: 915-828-3269

Guadalupe Mountains National Park is in west Texas about 100 miles east of El Paso. The park was established in 1972 and encompasses 86,190 acres of mountains and canyons. It contains the highest point in Texas, Guadalupe Peak at 8,749 feet. An entrance fee of $3 per person is charged.

Information is available from the Headquarters Visitor Center located just inside the park off US 62/180. The center is open 8:00 a.m. to 4:30 p.m. year-round. Exhibits feature the history of the area. Information is also available from a ranger station in Dog Canyon, which is 65 miles south of Carlsbad, New Mexico via NM 137.

There are two developed and ten backcountry campgrounds within the park. Campsites are available on a first-come, first-served basis; no reservations accepted. Backcountry camping requires a free permit that is available at the Headquarters Visitor Center or Dog Canyon Ranger Station. Over 80 miles of established trails exist within Guadalupe Mountains National Park. Water is available at trailheads only; none in the backcountry.

- **Dog Canyon**: at the park's northern entrance 65 miles south of Carlsbad via NM 137, open all year, four RV sites, nine tent sites, $8 per night, restrooms, drinking water, 14 day maximum stay, no fires (including charcoal) are allowed in the park.

- **Pine Springs**: located near Headquarters Visitor Center off US 62/180, open all year, 19 RV sites and 20 tent sites, $8 per night, drinking water, restrooms, public phone, 14 day maximum stay, no fires (including charcoal) are allowed in the park.

The following is a list of the ten backcountry campgrounds and the number of sites available. Contact the park for trail information and location of these campgrounds.

Name	Sites
Blue Ridge	5
Bush Mountain	5
Guadalupe Peak	5
Marcus	5
McKittrick Ridge	8
Mescalero	8
Pine Top	8
Shumard	5
Tejas	4
Wilderness Ridge	5

Lake Meredith National Recreation Area

PO Box 1460
Fritch, TX 79036
Phone: 806-857-3151
Fax: 806-857-2319

Lake Meredith National Recreation Area is in northern
Texas about 40 miles north of Amarillo. Construction of Sanford Dam
on the Canadian River created the lake. It was established in 1965 and
encompasses 44,977 acres. No entrance fee is charged.

Information is available from the park headquarters at 419 East
Broadway in Fritch. The office is open year-round from 8:00 a.m. to
4:30 p.m. Monday through Friday. It closes on federal holidays and
weekends. In summer it is open on weekends for boat permit sales.

There are 11 campgrounds within the national recreation area.
Campsites are available on a first-come, first-served basis. Obtain a
map from the visitor center to aid you in locating the following
campgrounds.

- **Blue Creek**: on west side of lake about ten miles from Sanford via Highways
  3395 and 1913, open all year, no designated campsites, no fee, chemical
  toilets, picnic tables, 14 day maximum stay. This area is one of two
  designated off-road vehicle areas. There is no drinking water.

- **Blue West**: on west side of lake about 14 miles from Sanford off Highway
  1913, open all year, designated sites, no camping fee, picnic tables, grills,
  vault toilets, boat ramp nearby, no water, 14 day stay limit.

- **Bugbee**: five miles from Sanford off Highway 3395, open all year, no
  designated campsites, no camping fee, picnic tables, chemical toilets, no
  water, 14 day maximum stay.

- **Cedar Canyon**: three miles from Sanford off Sanford-Yake Road, open all
  year, no designated sites, no fee, flush toilets, water, boat ramp, dump
  station, 14 day maximum stay.

- **Fritch Fortress**: four miles north of Fritch via Fritch Drive and El Paso Drive, open all year, individual campsites, no fee, picnic tables, grills, flush toilets, running water, boat ramp nearby, 14 day maximum stay.

- **Harbor Bay**: two miles west of Fritch via North Holmes Avenue and Lakeview Drive, open all year, no designated campsites, no camping fee, chemical toilets, boat ramp, some picnic tables, 14 day stay limit.

- **McBride Canyon**: seven miles south of Fritch on TX 136 and then six miles west, open all year, no designated sites, no fee, picnic tables, chemical toilet, no water, 14 day maximum stay. Access road can become impassable when wet.

- **Mullinaw**: located about three miles southwest of McBride Canyon Campground, open all year, individual sites, no fee, picnic tables, chemical toilets, no water, horseback riding, 14 day maximum stay.

- **Plum Creek**: on west side of lake 24 miles from Sanford south of Highway 1913, open all year, no designated sites, no fee, chemical toilets, picnic tables, no water, horseback riding trails, hiking and biking, 14 day maximum stay.

- **Rosita**: located along the Canadian River at the southern end of the park east of US 87/287, open all year, no designated campsites, no fee, chemical toilets, picnic tables, no water, 14 day maximum stay. This area is one of two designated off-road vehicle areas.

- **Sanford-Yake**: four miles west of Sanford via Sanford-Yake Road, open all year, individual sites, no fee, picnic tables, flush toilets, running water, grills, dump station, 14 day stay limit. A marina and boat ramp is nearby.

Padre Island National Seashore

PO Box 181300
Corpus Christi, TX 78480
Phone: 361-949-8173 or 361-949-8068
Fax: 361-949-8023

Padre Island National Seashore is in southern Texas, southeast of Corpus Christi. It was established in 1962 and preserves 133,000 acres of barrier islands. It is the longest remaining undeveloped barrier island in the world. An entrance fee of $10 is charged and is good for seven days.

Information is available from the Malaquite Beach Visitor Center, open daily from 8:30 a.m. to 4:30 p.m. in winter. Summer hours are extended to 6:00 p.m. The center is closed on Christmas and New Year's Day. Exhibits detail the park's natural history. A small museum displays the island's human and natural history.

There are five camping areas within the park. Campsites are available on a first-come, first-served basis. A camping permit is required and is available for free at the visitor center or the Malaquite campground host.

- **Bird Island Basin**: primitive camping on Laguna Madre about four miles northwest of visitor center, open all year, suitable for RVs and tents, $5 per night or purchase an annual pass for $10, chemical toilets, 14 day maximum stay. This area is used primarily for boat launching and windsurfing.

- **Malaquite**: one-half mile from visitor center, open all year, 16 RV sites, 26 RV/tent sites, eight tent-only sites, $8 per night, restrooms, cold showers, picnic tables, dump station, 14 day maximum stay.

- **North Beach**: one-mile stretch of beach at the northern end of the park, primitive camping open to RVs and tents, open all year, no designated sites, no camping fee, no facilities, 14 day maximum stay.

- **South Beach**: defined as the 60-mile stretch from the end of Park Road 22 to the southern end of the park, open all year, no designated sites, no fees, no facilities, 14 day maximum stay. The first five miles of beach are usually suitable for two-wheel-drive vehicles. Many RVers stay in this area during winter. The remaining 55 miles require the use of a four-wheel-drive vehicle. In Texas, beaches are considered highways and all vehicles on them must be street-legal and licensed. Check with the visitor center for beach conditions before driving down the island.

- **Yarborough Pass**: primitive camping on Laguna Madre about 16 miles south of visitor center, open all year, no facilities, no designated sites, no camping fee, 14 day maximum stay. The camping area is only accessible by four-wheel-drive vehicles.

Utah

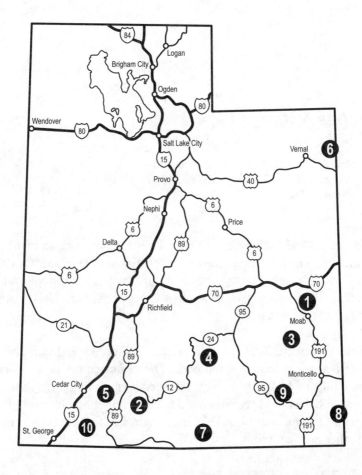

Activities Chart

Park	🚗	🚲	🥾	🐴	🚶	🛶	🦆	🎿	➤	✕	⛷	🛶
1	•	•	•		•							
2	•		•	•	•						•	•
3	•	•	•	•	•	•		•				
4	•	•	•	•	•		•			•		
5	•		•		•						•	•
7	•	•	•			•	•	•	•	•		
8		•		•								
9	•		•		•							
10		•	•								•	

Arches National Park

PO Box 907
Moab, UT 84532
Phone: 435-719-2299 or 435-719-2100
Fax: 435-719-2305

Arches National Park is in southeast Utah five miles north of Moab. Proclaimed a national monument in 1929, it was re-designated in 1971. It consists of nearly 80,000 acres and 2,000 natural sandstone arches, including the famous Delicate Arch. An entrance fee of $10 is charged and is good for seven days.

Information is available from the Arches Visitor Center located along US 191 at the entrance to the park. The visitor center is open daily from 8:00 a.m. to 4:30 p.m. with extended hours spring through fall. It closes on Christmas Day. Features include a museum with exhibits on the park's natural and cultural history. A sales area features books, maps, and other publications.

There is one campground within the park. Campsites are available on a first-come, first-served basis only; no reservations are accepted. Visitors must pre-register for campsites at the visitor center or entrance station. The campground usually fills early. Wood gathering is prohibited; bring your own wood or charcoal.

- **Devils Garden**: 18 miles north of the park entrance, open all year, 52 RV/ tent sites, $10 per night mid-March to late October, $5 per night rest of year, flush toilets and water spring through fall, limited facilities in winter, picnic tables, grills, 30-foot RV length limit, 14 day maximum stay.

Bryce Canyon National Park

PO Box 170001
Bryce Canyon, UT 84717
Phone: 435-834-5322

Bryce Canyon National Park is in south-central Utah about 70 miles east of Cedar City. Established in 1923, the park encompasses 35,835 acres of colorful and unique rock formations. An entrance fee of $20 is charged and is good for seven days.

Information is available from the visitor center along the park road. It is open year-round except on Thanksgiving Day, Christmas Day, and New Year's Day. Hours vary by season but are generally 8:00 a.m. to 8:00 p.m. A museum has displays of geology, wildlife, and historic and prehistoric culture.

There are two developed campgrounds in the park. Campsites are available on a first-come, first-served basis; no reservations accepted. Backcountry camping is allowed on a limited basis and only at designated sites. A backcountry permit is required and can be obtained at the visitor center; the cost is $5. Motel rooms and cabins are available at Bryce Canyon Lodge.

- **North**: located east of the visitor center, open all year, 110 RV/tent sites, some pull-thrus, $10 per night, picnic tables, drinking water, restrooms, showers nearby, dump station, groceries, laundry facilities, 30-foot RV length limit, 14 day maximum stay.

- **Sunset**: two miles south of visitor center, open late April to mid-October, 100 RV/tent sites, $10 per night, picnic tables, drinking water, restrooms, showers nearby, 30-foot RV length limit, 14 day maximum stay.

Canyonlands National Park

2282 S West Resource Blvd
Moab, UT 84532
Phone: 435-719-2313
Fax: 435-719-2300

Canyonlands National Park is in southeast Utah, southwest of Moab. The park was established in 1964 and consists of 337,570 acres. Among the park's features are prehistoric Indian rock art and ruins. An entrance fee of $10 per vehicle is charged and is good for seven days.

Information is available from two visitor centers. Island In The Sky Visitor Center is in the park's northern area and is 32 miles from Moab via US 191 and UT 313. It is open year-round from 8:00 a.m. to 4:30 p.m. Needles District Visitor Center is in the southern area of the park and is 76 miles from Moab via US 191 and UT 211. It is also open all year between 8:00 a.m. and 4:30 p.m. Both centers close on Christmas Day and feature exhibits of the area's natural and cultural history.

There are two campgrounds in the park. Campsites are available on a first-come, first-served basis. Primitive backcountry campsites and backpacking zones exist in each district of the park. These sites are accessible by foot, four-wheel-drive vehicle or boat. Permits are required and may be reserved in advance. Other camping options include Dead Horse Point State Park and nearby Bureau of Land Management campgrounds.

- **Squaw Flat**: located in the Needles District west of the visitor center, open all year, 26 campsites, $10 per night, restrooms, picnic tables, fire grates, drinking water, 28-foot RV length limit, seven day maximum stay.

- **Willow Flat**: six miles south of Island In The Sky Visitor Center, open all year, 12 sites, $5 per night, picnic tables, fire grates, vault toilets, no drinking water, 28-foot RV length limit, seven day maximum stay.

Capitol Reef National Park

HC 70 Box 15
Torrey, UT 84775
Phone: 435-425-3791
Fax: 435-425-3026

Capitol Reef National Park is in south-central Utah about 130 miles northeast of Cedar City. It was established in 1937 and encompasses 243,559 acres. The park preserves the 100-mile-long Waterpocket Fold, an uplift of sandstone cliffs. There is an entrance fee of $5 per vehicle for traveling the park's scenic drive beyond the Fruita campground. The entrance fee is good for seven days.

Information is available from the Capitol Reef Visitor Center located ten miles east of Torrey off UT 24. The center is open year-round, except on Christmas Day, between 8:00 a.m. and 4:30 p.m. Hours are extended during summer. A museum offers an overview of the park's features and exhibits on geology, archeology, and history.

There are three campgrounds in the park. Campsites are available on a first-come, first-served basis. Backcountry camping is allowed. A permit is required and is available free at the visitor center.

- **Cathedral Valley**: 18 miles east of Fremont via UT 72 and Forest Service Road 206, open all year, six sites, no fee, pit toilets, picnic tables, fire grates, no drinking water. A high-clearance, four-wheel-drive vehicle is recommended to reach the campground.

- **Cedar Mesa**: 35 miles south of visitor center via UT 24 and Notom-Bullfrog Road, open all year, five sites, primitive camping, no fee, picnic tables, fire grates, pit toilets, no drinking water.

- **Fruita**: one mile south of visitor center off Scenic Drive, open all year, 70 RV/tent sites, $10 per night, picnic tables, restrooms, drinking water, dump station, amphitheater, 14 day maximum stay.

Cedar Breaks National Monument

2390 W Hwy 56, Suite 11
Cedar City, UT 84720
Phone: 435-586-9451
Fax: 435-586-3813

Cedar Breaks National Monument preserves a huge natural amphitheater that has been eroded out of the multicolored Pink Cliffs near Cedar City, Utah. The canyon spans some three miles and is over 2,000 feet deep. An entrance fee of $3 is charged and is good for seven days.

Information is available from the Cedar Breaks Visitor Center on UT 148. The center is open from late May to mid-October, hours vary. A two-mile hiking trail begins here that will take you to some panoramic overlooks.

Camping is available in one campground. Campsites are available on a first-come, first-served basis. Campfires are allowed in designated fire pits but campers must provide their own firewood.

- **Point Supreme**: about 20 miles east of Cedar City via UT 14 and UT 148, open mid-June through September, 30 sites, $12 per night, 35-foot RV length limit, picnic tables, grills, water, flush toilets, 14 day stay limit.

Glen Canyon National Recreation Area

PO Box 1507
Page, AZ 86040
Phone: 928-608-6404 or 928-608-6200
Fax: 928-608-6283

Glen Canyon National Recreation Area is in southern Utah and northern Arizona. The 1,252,246-acre recreation area was established in 1972. Lake Powell stretches 186 miles behind Glen Canyon Dam and is the park's main attraction. An entrance fee of $10 per vehicle is charged and is good for seven days.

Information is available from two visitor centers. Bullfrog Visitor Center is 86 miles south of Hanksville via UT 95 and UT 276. It is open April to late October. Carl Hayden Visitor Center is located at Glen Canyon Dam on US 89 in Page, Arizona. It is open all year between 8:00 a.m. and 5:00 p.m. Hours are extended in summer. Dam tours are offered. Information is also available from the Hans Flat Ranger Station and Hite Ranger Station.

In addition to the campgrounds listed below, there are seven primitive campgrounds that have no facilities other than pit toilets. These are as follows: Lone Rock, Stanton Creek, Bullfrog North, Bullfrog South, Hite, Dirty Devil, and Farley Canyon. The camping fee is $6 per night. Obtain a map from one of the visitor centers to locate these. Backcountry camping is also allowed.

- **Lees Ferry**: National Park Service campground in Arizona five miles north of Marble Canyon off Alternate US 89, open all year, 51 sites, $12 per night, flush toilets, 35-foot RV length limit, 14 day maximum stay, boat ramp nearby.

- **Bullfrog**: concessionaire-operated campground in Utah about 86 miles south of Hanksville via UT 95 and UT 276, open all year, 40 tent sites, 85 RV/tent sites, $18 per night, 14 day maximum stay, 40-foot RV length limit. Nearby facilities: dump station, hot showers, laundry, gas, boat ramp, marina, restaurant, and lodging.

- **Bullfrog RV Park (Painted Hills)**: concessionaire-operated campground in Utah about 86 miles south of Hanksville via UT 95 and UT 276, open all year, 24 RV sites with full hookups, $29 per night, 14 day maximum stay, pull-thru spaces (20) can accommodate RVs up to 45 feet, back-in spaces (4) can accommodate RVs up to 35 feet. Nearby facilities: dump station, hot showers, laundry, gas, boat ramp, marina, restaurant, and lodging.

- **Halls Crossing**: concessionaire-operated campground in Utah 87 miles west of Blanding via UT 95 and UT 276, open year-round, 32 RV sites with full hookups ($29 per night), 60 tent sites ($18 per night), hot showers, flush toilets, dump station, laundry facilities, groceries, 14 day maximum stay. RV sites can accommodate RVs up to 60 feet. Nearby facilities: boat ramp and marina.

- **Wahweap**: concessionaire-operated campground in Arizona four miles north of Glen Canyon Dam off US 89, open all year, 179 sites, $18 per night, 14 day maximum stay, 45-foot RV length limit.

- **Wahweap RV Park**: concessionaire-operated campground in Arizona four miles north of Glen Canyon Dam off US 89, open all year, 100 RV sites with complete hookups, $29 per night, 45-foot RV length limit, 14 day maximum stay, dump station, showers, laundry, groceries. Marina and boat ramp nearby.

Hovenweep National Monument

McElmo Route
Cortez, CO 81321
Phone: 970-562-4282 or 435-719-2100

Hovenweep National Monument is in southeast Utah about 37 miles southeast of Blanding. Established in 1923, the monument preserves a collection of unique prehistoric archeological sites. Some of the sites are in Colorado. An entrance fee of $6 per vehicle is charged and is good for seven days.

Information is available from the visitor center along Hovenweep Road. The center is open all year between 8:00 a.m. and 4:00 p.m. and has limited exhibits and educational information. Hours are extended in summer. It closes on winter holidays. There is a small sales area with books on the culture and natural history of the area.

There is one campground in the park. Campsites are available on a first-come, first-served basis. Some roads to the monument are rough and can become impassable in inclement weather.

- **Hovenweep**: located near the visitor center, open all year, 31 sites, $10 per night, flush toilets, running water, 14 day maximum stay. The campsites are designed for tent camping but a few will accommodate RVs of 25 feet or less. Limited facilities in winter.

Natural Bridges National Monument

HC 60 Box 1
Lake Powell, UT 84533
Phone: 435-692-1234 or 435-719-2100
Fax: 435-692-1111

Natural Bridges National Monument is in southeast Utah about 40 miles west of Blanding via UT 95 and UT 275. It was established in 1908 and encompasses 7,636 acres. Features include three natural bridges carved out of sandstone and ancient Indian rock art and ruins. An entrance fee of $6 is charged that is good for seven days.

Information is available from the Natural Bridges Visitor Center at the end of UT 275. It remains open all year except on Christmas Day. Hours are 8:00 a.m. to 5:00 p.m. An orientation video is shown on request. Exhibits highlight natural and cultural history of the area.

There is one small campground in the monument. Campsites are available on a first-come, first-served basis. Visitors must bring their own wood for campfires as wood gathering is prohibited. Water is available at the visitor center but not at the campground.

- **Natural Bridges**: open all year, 13 sites, $10 per night, picnic tables, fire grates, 26-foot RV length limit, 14 day maximum stay. The campground fills by early afternoon from March through October. Snow is not removed from roads during winter.

Zion National Park

State Route 9
Springdale, UT 84767
Phone: 435-772-3256
Fax: 435-772-3426

Zion National Park is in southwest Utah about 55 miles
south of Cedar City. The park was established in 1919 and encompasses
143,035 acres of colorful canyon and mesa scenery. An entrance fee of
$20 per vehicle is charged and is good for seven days.

Information is available from two visitor centers. Kolob Canyons Visitor
Center is in the northern part of the park east of I-15 at Exit 40. Zion
Canyon Visitor Center is near the south entrance to the park along UT
9. Both are open daily from 8:00 a.m. to 7:00 p.m. in summer. Hours
are shortened during winter.

There are three campgrounds in the park. Backcountry camping is also
available. Permits are required for all backcountry camping. The cost
is $5 per person. Campsites in Lava Point and South Campgrounds are
available on a first-come, first-served basis. Reservations are accepted
for campsites in Watchman Campground (call 1-800-365-2267).
Lodging available at Zion Lodge off Zion Canyon Scenic Drive.

- **Lava Point**: 27 miles south of I-15 Exit #51 via Kolob Reservoir Road,
  open June to November, six primitive sites, no water, no camping fee,
  maximum vehicle size is 19 feet. Access roads impassable when wet.

- **South**: located south of the visitor center off UT 9, open year-round, 128
  RV/tent sites, $14 per night, flush toilets, dump station, amphitheater, picnic
  tables, fire grates, running water, 14 day maximum stay.

- **Watchman**: off UT 9 south of the visitor center, open all year, 91 RV sites
  with electric hookups ($16 per night), 69 tent sites at $14 per night, picnic
  tables, fire grates, running water, flush toilets, dump station, amphitheater,
  14 day maximum stay.

Virgin Islands

1 Virgin Islands National Park

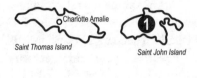

Saint Thomas Island

Saint John Island

Saint Croix Island

Frederiksted Christiansted

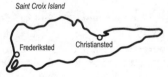

Activities Chart

Park

1

Virgin Islands National Park

1300 Cruz Bay Creek
Saint John, VI 00830
Phone: 340-776-6201
Fax: 340-775-9592

Virgin Islands National Park is on the island of Saint John. Nearly all of Hassel Island in Charlotte Amalie Harbor on Saint Thomas is included as part of the national park. The park was established in 1956 and consists of 12,909 acres. Features include coral reefs, quiet coves, blue-green waters, and white sandy beaches fringed by green hills. No entrance fee is charged but a $4 user fee is collected at Annaberg and Trunk Bay.

Information is available from the Cruz Bay Visitor Center across from the ferry dock in Cruz Bay. The visitor center is open all year from 8:00 a.m. to 4:30 p.m. It closes on Christmas Day. Maps, brochures, and the latest activity schedule are available from park rangers.

There is one campground in the park. Campground reservations in winter months should be made four to six months in advance by calling 340-776-6330. Backcountry or beach camping is not allowed.

- **Cinnamon Bay**: open all year, 26 tent sites ($27 per night), 44 sites with tent-covered platforms ($80 per night), 40 cottages ($110 to $140 per night), restrooms, showers, phones, camp store, restaurant. Cottages and tent-covered sites are equipped with cooking supplies and linens. Rates are lower in off-season (May through mid-December).

Virginia

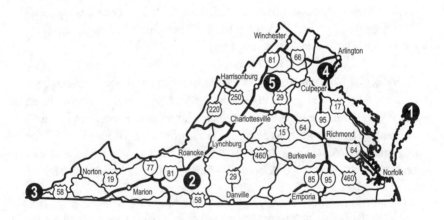

Activities Chart

Park	🚙	🚲	🥾	🐎	🧗	🛶	🦆	🏄	🏊	✖	⛷	🛷
4	•	•	•		•		•			•	•	
5	•	•	•	•	•		•			•		

Prince William Forest Park

18100 Park Headquarters Road
Triangle, VA 22172
Phone: 703-221-4706 or 703-221-7181
Fax: 703-221-4322

Prince William Forest Park is in northeast Virginia approximately 30 miles southwest of Arlington. The park was established in 1933 and encompasses 17,500 acres of pine and hardwood forests. A $5 entrance fee is charged and is good for three days.

Information is available from the visitor center located along the park road, which is accessed from I-95 at Exit 150. The center is open all year from 8:30 a.m. to 5:00 p.m. It closes on Thanksgiving Day, Christmas Day, and New Year's Day.

There is one National Park Service campground and one operated by a concessionaire. Campsites at Oak Ridge Campground are available on a first-come, first-served basis. Travel Trailer Village, the concessionaire-operated campground, accepts reservations; call 703-221-2474 for information. Also available are five cabins built in the 1930s that can accommodate up to 200 people. For information call 703-221-5843.

- **Oak Ridge**: in the western portion of the park off the scenic drive, 100 sites, $10 per night, picnic tables, fire grills, drinking water, flush toilets, showers, amphitheater, 14 day maximum stay, 32-foot RV length limit.

- **Travel Trailer Village**: located on the north side of the park via VA 234 from I-95 Exit 152, concessionaire operated, open all year, 74 RV sites with electric and water hookups, 29 sites also have sewer hookups, $21 to $24 per night, swimming pool, hot showers, flush toilets, dump station, laundry facilities, 35-foot RV length limit, 14 day maximum stay.

Shenandoah National Park

3655 US Highway 211E
Luray, VA 22835
Phone: 540-999-3500
Fax: 540-999-3601

Shenandoah National Park is in northern Virginia between Front Royal and Charlottesville. It was established in 1935 and covers 197,038 acres. Among the park's features is Skyline Drive, which winds along the crest of the Blue Ridge Mountains for 105 miles. An entrance fee of $10 is charged that is good for seven days.

Information is available from two visitor centers and one information center. Dickey Ridge Visitor Center is located near milepost five on Skyline Drive (milepost 0 is at the northern end of the park). Harry F. Byrd, Sr. Visitor Center is located at milepost 51 on Skyline Drive. Both visitor centers are open daily. Loft Mountain Information Center is near milepost 80 on Skyline Drive.

There are four campgrounds in Shenandoah National Park. Only one accepts reservations, Big Meadows Campground (800-365-2267). All other campground sites are available on a first-come, first-served basis.

- **Mathews Arm**: at milepost 22.1 on Skyline Drive, open spring through October, 179 campsites, $16 per night, picnic tables, grills, dump station, 14 day maximum stay.

- **Big Meadows**: located at milepost 51.3, open spring through November, 217 campsites, $19 per night, reservations required mid-May through November (1-800-365-2267), picnic tables, grills, amphitheater, showers, laundry facilities, campstore, dump station, 14 day maximum stay.

- **Lewis Mountain**: at milepost 57.5 on Skyline Drive, open spring through October, 32 sites, $16 per night, picnic tables, grills, showers, laundry facilities, amphitheater, campstore, cabins available, 14 day maximum stay.

- **Loft Mountain**: at milepost 79.5 on Skyline Drive, open spring through October, 219 sites, $16 per night, picnic tables, grills, showers, dump station, laundry facilities, campstore, amphitheater, 14 day maximum stay.

Washington

1   Lake Roosevelt National Recreation Area
2   Mount Rainier National Park
3   North Cascades National Park
      Lake Chelan National Recreation Area
      Ross Lake National Recreation Area
4   Olympic National Park

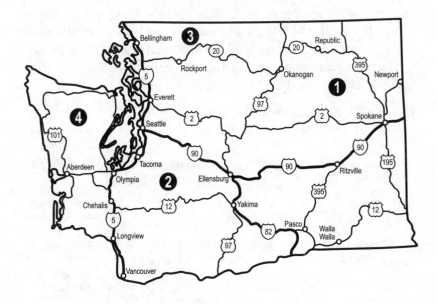

Activities Chart

Park	🚐	🚲	🥾	🐴	🚶	🌊	🦆	⛷	🏊	✈	⛷	🛶
1	•		•		•	•	•	•	•	•	•	
2	•	•	•	•	•		•					•
3	•	•	•	•	•	•	•	•			•	•
4	•	•	•	•	•	•	•	•	•	•		•

Lake Roosevelt National Recreation Area

1008 Crest Dr
Coulee Dam, WA 99116
Phone: 509-633-9441 or 509-738-6266
Fax: 509-633-9332

Lake Roosevelt National Recreation Area is in northeast Washington between Coulee Dam and Kettle Falls. It was established in 1946 and consists of 100,390 acres. The principal attraction is 130-mile long Franklin D. Roosevelt Lake. There is no entrance fee.

Information is available from the Fort Spokane Museum and Visitor Center. It is located on WA 25 near Two Rivers Casino, 22 miles north of Davenport. The center is open from Memorial Day Weekend to mid-September. Features include Fort Spokane, which was converted to an Indian boarding school after the military left in 1899.

There are 27 campgrounds in the recreation area; some are only accessed by boat. All campsites are available on a first-come, first-served basis.

- **Cloverleaf**: boat-in or walk-in campground near Gifford, open all year, nine sites, vault toilets, water, boat dock, no camping fee.

- **Crystal Cove**: boat-in campground on the Spokane River Arm, open all year, three sites, vault toilets, no water, no camping fee.

- **Detillion**: boat-in campground on the Spokane River Arm, open all year, 12 sites, vault toilets, water, boat dock, no camping fee.

- **Enterprise**: boat-in campground between mile 55 and 60, open all year, 13 sites, vault toilets, no water, no camping fee.

- **Evans**: one mile south of Evans along WA 25, open all year, 43 RV/tent sites, $10 per night May through September, $5 per night rest of year, flush toilets, drinking water, boat ramp, boat dock, dump station, amphitheater, 14 day maximum stay.

- **Fort Spokane**: 21 miles north of Davenport on WA 25, 67 RV/tent sites, $10 per night May through September, $5 per night rest of year, flush toilets, drinking water, boat ramp, boat dock, dump station, amphitheater, 14 day maximum stay.

- **Gifford**: two miles south of Gifford along WA 25, open all year, 42 RV/tent sites, $10 per night May through September, $5 per night rest of year, vault toilets, water, boat ramp, boat dock, dump station, 14 day stay limit.

- **Goldsmith**: boat-in campground between mile 15 and 20, open all year, three sites, vault toilets, no water, no camping fee.

- **Haag Cove**: eight miles southwest of Kettle Falls via WA 20 and County Road 3, open all year, 16 sites, $10 per night May through September, $5 per night rest of year, vault toilets, water, boat dock, 14 day maximum stay.

- **Halversen Canyon**: boat-in campground near mile 30, open all year, one site, vault toilet, no water, no camping fee.

- **Hawk Creek**: 13 miles east of Creston via US 2 and Miles Creston Road, open all year, 21 sites, $10 per night May through September, $5 per night rest of year, vault toilets, water, boat ramp, boat dock, 14 day stay limit.

- **Hunters**: two miles west of Hunters off WA 25, open all year, 39 RV/tent sites, $10 per night May through September, $5 per night rest of year, flush toilets, water, boat ramp, boat dock, dump station, 14 day stay limit.

- **Jones Bay**: 18 miles north of Wilbur via WA 21 and local roads, open all year, nine sites, $10 per night May through September, $5 per night rest of year, vault toilets, no drinking water, boat ramp and dock, 14 day stay limit.

- **Kamloops**: seven miles northwest of Kettle Falls via US 395, open all year, 17 sites, $10 per night May through September, $5 per night rest of year, vault toilets, water, boat dock, 14 day maximum stay.

- **Keller Ferry**: 15 miles north of Wilbur via WA 21, open all year, 55 campsites, $10 per night May through September, $5 per night rest of year, flush toilets, drinking water, boat ramp, boat dock, marina, dump station, 14 day maximum stay.

- **Kettle Falls**: four miles west of Kettle Falls via Old Kettle Road, open year-round, 76 RV/tent sites, $10 per night May through September, $5 per night rest of year, flush toilets, drinking water, marina, boat ramp, boat dock, dump station, 14 day maximum stay.

- **Kettle River**: ten miles north of Kettle Falls via US 395, open all year, 13 sites, $10 per night May through September, $5 per night rest of year, vault toilets, water, boat dock, 14 day maximum stay.

- **Marcus Island**: seven miles north of Kettle Falls via WA 25, open year-round, 27 sites, $10 per night May through September, $5 per night rest of year, vault toilets, drinking water, boat dock and ramp, 14 day stay limit.

- **North Gorge**: 18 miles north of Kettle Falls off WA 25, year-round, 12 sites, $10 per night May through September, $5 per night rest of year, vault toilets, water, boat ramp, boat dock, 14 day maximum stay.

- **Penix**: boat-in campground between mile 20 and 25, open all year, three sites, no camping fee, vault toilets, no drinking water.

- **Plum Point**: boat-in campground between mile 5 and 10, open all year, four sites, no fee, vault toilets, boat dock, no drinking water.

- **Ponderosa**: boat-in campground on Spokane River Arm, open year-round, eight sites, vault toilets, no drinking water, no fee.

- **Porcupine Bay**: 18 miles north of Davenport via WA 25 and Porcupine Bay Road, open all year, 31 campsites, $10 per night May through September, $5 per night rest of year, flush toilets, water, boat ramp, boat dock, dump station, 14 day maximum stay.

- **Snag Cove**: eight miles northeast of Kamloops Campground via Northport Flat Creek Road, open year-round, nine sites, $10 per night May through September, $5 per night rest of year, vault toilets, water, boat ramp, boat dock, 14 day maximum stay.

- **Spring Canyon**: three miles east of Grand Coulee via WA 174, open all year, 87 sites, $10 per night May through September, $5 per night rest of year, flush toilets, water, boat ramp, boat dock, dump station, 14 day maximum stay.

- **Sterling Point**: boat-in campground between mile 30 and 35, open all year, five sites, no fee, vault toilets, no drinking water.

- **Summer Island**: boat-in campground near mile 110, six sites, vault toilets, boat dock, no water, no camping fee.

Mount Rainier National Park

Tahoma Woods, Star Route
Ashford, WA 98304
Phone: 360-569-2211
Fax: 360-569-2170

Mount Rainier National Park is in west-central Washington about one hundred miles southeast of Olympia. The park was established in 1899 and encompasses 235,625 acres. About 97 percent of the park is designated wilderness. An entrance fee of $10 per vehicle is charged and is good for seven days.

Information is available from three visitor centers. Jackson Visitor Center is in Paradise off the main park road. It is open daily late May to mid-October. Features include exhibits on the natural and cultural history of the park. Ohanapecosh Visitor Center is in the southeast corner of the park off WA 123. It is also open late May to mid-October. Sunrise Visitor Center is open July to mid-October and is located in the northeast corner of the park on Sunrise Park Road.

There are six National Park Service campgrounds. Reservations are required for campsites in Cougar Rock and Ohanapecosh between late June and Labor Day. Otherwise, all campsites are available on a first-come, first-served basis. Lodging is also available at National Park Inn or Paradise Inn.

- **Cougar Rock**: southwest corner of park just over two miles north of Longmire, open late May to mid-October, 173 sites, $15 per night during reservation season, $12 per night rest of year, 35-foot RV length limit (27 feet for trailers), water, flush toilets, dump station, fire grates, picnic tables, amphitheater, hiking trails, 14 day maximum stay. Reservations required late June to Labor Day, call 800-365-2267.

- **Ipsut Creek**: in the northwest corner of park five miles east of Carbon River Entrance, open all year, 30 sites, $10 per night, picnic tables, vault toilets, no potable water, 14 day maximum stay. Access road to campground is rough; RVers may have difficulty.

- **Mowich Lake**: in the northwest corner of park at end of WA 165, open July to mid-October, undesignated walk-in sites, pit toilets, no potable water, no camping fee.

- **Ohanapecosh**: 11 miles northeast of Packwood on WA 123 in the southeast corner of park, open late May to mid-October, 188 RV/tent sites, $15 per night during reservation season, $12 per night rest of season, drinking water, flush toilets, dump station, amphitheater, picnic tables, fire grates, hiking trails, 14 day maximum stay. Reservations required from late June to Labor Day, call 800-365-2267.

- **Sunshine Point**: seven miles east of Ashford on WA 706, open all year, 18 sites, $10 per night, water, vault toilets, picnic tables, fire grates, 14 day maximum stay.

- **White River**: five miles west of White River Entrance off WA 410, open late June through September, 112 sites, $10 per night, drinking water, flush toilets, picnic tables, fire grates, amphitheater, dump station, 14 day maximum stay.

North Cascades National Park

810 State Route 20
Sedro-Woolley, WA 98284
Phone: 360-856-5700
Fax: 360-856-1934

North Cascades National Park is in northern Washington. It was established in 1968 and is 684,242 acres in size. Within the park are two national recreation areas: Ross Lake and Lake Chelan. Over 93 percent of the three areas are included in the Stephen Mather Wilderness. No entrance fees are charged.

Information is available from the park headquarters in Sedro-Woolley on WA 20. Hours vary but the office is open year-round. Information can also be obtained from two visitor centers. Golden West Visitor Center is at Stehekin Landing near the north end of Lake Chelan. There is no road access to Golden West. North Cascades Visitor Center is along WA 20 near the town of Newhalem. It remains open year-round.

There are four vehicle-accessible campgrounds in the Ross Lake National Recreation Area. Campsites are available on a first-come, first-served basis. All of the campgrounds in Lake Chelan National Recreation Area are primitive, backcountry campsites. A wilderness permit, available free of charge, is required. Lodging is also available at North Cascades Stehekin Lodge and Ross Lake Resort. The vehicle-accessible campgrounds are described below.

- **Colonial Creek**: ten miles east of Newhalem on WA 20, open mid-May to mid-October, 147 sites, $12 per night, picnic tables, fire rings, drinking water, flush toilets, dump station, boat ramp, trails, 14 day stay limit. Winter camping permitted in main parking area but any snow is not removed.

- **Goodell Creek**: one mile west of Newhalem on WA 20, open all year, 21 sites, no large RVs, $10 per night, picnic tables, fire rings, vault toilets, drinking water, 14 day maximum stay.

- **Hozomeen**: at north end of Ross Lake south of U.S./Canada border, open mid-May through October, 122 sites, no camping fee, picnic tables, fire rings, drinking water, vault toilets, 14 day maximum stay. This campground can only be reached by following Silver-Skagit Road, a gravel surfaced road, for 40 miles from Hope, British Columbia in Canada.

- **Newhalem Creek**: on WA 20 in Newhalem, open mid-April to mid-October, 111 sites, $12 per night, no RV length limit, picnic tables, fire rings, drinking water, flush toilets, dump station, 14 day maximum stay.

Following is a list of 19 campgrounds on Ross Lake that are accessed only by boat, hiking, or horseback. All campsites are equipped with fire rings, picnic tables, and vault toilets. A backcountry permit is required. A boat ramp is at the north end of Ross Lake in Hozomeen, which is only reached by a gravel road from Hope, British Columbia.

Campground	Miles from Hozomeen	Number of sites
Green Point	21.4	5
Cougar Island	19.7	2
Roland Point	18.1	1
McMillan	17.8	3
Big Beaver	17.6	7
Spencer's	17.7	2
May Creek	17.2	1
Rainbow Point	15.9	3
Devils Junction	12.9	1
Ten Mile Island	12.2	3
Dry Creek	11.8	4
Ponderosa	11.2	2
Lodgepole	10.7	3
Lightning Creek Horse	10.4	3
Lightning Creek Boat	10.2	6
Cat Island	9.2	4
Little Beaver	7.0	5
Boundary Bay	5.7	3
Silver Creek	1.9	3

In Lake Chelan National Recreation Area there are 11 campgrounds in Stehekin Valley, which is accessible by boat, floatplane, foot, or horseback. A National Park Service shuttle bus does travel the valley two times a day during the summer and fall (reservations required). All campsites in Stehekin Valley require a permit, which is available free. The following is a list of the campgrounds and number of sites: Purple Point (7), Harlequin (6), Bullion (2), High Bridge (2), Tumwater (2), Dolly Varden (2), Shady (1), Bridge Creek (6), Park Creek (2), Flat Creek (4), Cottonwood (4).

There are three lakeside campgrounds on Lake Chelan within the recreation area. A $5 docking permit is required. Campground names and number of sites follow: Weaver Point (22), Manly Wham (1), Flick Creek (1).

Olympic National Park

600 E Park Ave
Port Angeles, WA 98362
Phone: 360-565-3130 or 360-565-3131
Fax: 360-565-3015

Olympic National Park is in northwest Washington about 100 miles northwest of Olympia. It was established in 1938 and encompasses 913,339 acres. Among its features are glacier-capped mountains, valleys, meadows, lakes, and miles of beaches. An entrance fee of $10 is charged and is good for seven days.

Information is available from three visitor centers. The main visitor center is in Port Angeles off US 101. It is open year-round. Hurricane Ridge Visitor Center is south of Port Angeles along Heart O' the Hills Road. It is open year-round but may not be staffed in winter. The Hoh Rain Forest Visitor Center also remains open year-round but may not be staffed in winter. It is located on Upper Hoh Road about 16 miles east of US 101.

The National Park Service operates 16 campgrounds. All campsites are available on a first-come, first-served basis except for sites in Kalaloch, which operates on a reservation system in summer. Lodging is available at Kalaloch Lodge, Lake Crescent Lodge, Log Cabin Resort, and Sol Duc Hot Springs Resort.

- **Altaire**: 13 miles southwest of Port Angeles via US 101 and Olympic Hot Springs Road, open May to October, 30 sites, $10 per night, water, flush toilets, picnic tables, fire pit or grill, 21-foot RV length limit, 14 day stay limit. Campground subject to closure during low visitor use periods.

- **Deer Park**: 22 miles southeast of Port Angeles via US 101 and Deer Park Road, open May to October, 14 tent sites, $8 per night, water, pit toilets, picnic tables, fire pit or grill, 14 day maximum stay. Campground subject to closure during low visitor use periods.

- **Dosewallips**: 15 miles west of Brinnon on Dosewallips Road, open June through September, 30 walk-in sites, pit toilets, no water, picnic tables, fire pit or grill, nature trails, 14 day maximum stay. Part of access road to campground was washed out in 2002 and remains closed. Campers must hike 5 miles to reach the campground.

- **Elwha**: 12 miles southwest of Port Angeles via US 101 and Olympic Hot Springs Road, open all year, 40 sites, $10 per night, water, restrooms, picnic tables, fire pit or grill, 21-foot RV length limit, 14 day maximum stay. Limited facilities in winter.

- **Fairholm**: 26 miles west of Port Angeles on US 101, open May to October, 88 sites, some pull-thrus, $10 per night, water, restrooms, dump station, picnic tables, fire pit or grill, boat ramp, restaurant, 21-foot RV length limit, 14 day maximum stay. Campground subject to closure during low visitor use periods.

- **Graves Creek**: 20 miles east of Amanda Park on Quinault River Road, 30 sites, $10 per night, water, restrooms, picnic tables, fire pit or grill, nature trails, 21-foot RV length limit, 14 day maximum stay. Campground subject to closure during low visitor use periods.

- **Heart O' the Hills**: five miles south of Port Angeles on Heart O' the Hills Road, open all year, 105 sites, $10 per night, water, restrooms, picnic tables, fire pit or grill, nature trails, 21-foot RV length limit, 14 day stay limit.

- **Hoh**: on Hoh River Road near visitor center, open year-round, 88 sites, $10 per night, water, restrooms, dump station, picnic tables, fire pit or grill, 21-foot RV length limit, 14 day maximum stay.

- **Kalaloch**: 35 miles south of Forks on US 101, open all year, 175 sites, $16 per night mid-June to early September, $12 per night rest of year, water, flush toilets, dump station, picnic tables, fire pit or grill, 21-foot RV length limit, 14 day maximum stay. Reservations accepted (800-365-2267).

- **Mora**: 14 miles west of Forks on Mora Road via WA 110, open all year, 94 sites, some pull-thrus, $10 per night, water, restrooms, dump station, picnic tables, fire pit or grill, 21-foot RV length limit, 14 day maximum stay.

- **North Fork**: 20 miles northeast of Amanda Park via North Shore Road, seven tent sites, no camping fee, pit toilets, picnic tables, fire pit or grill, 14 day stay limit. Campground subject to closure during low visitor use periods.

- **Ozette**: 24 miles southwest of Sekiu via WA 112 and Hoko Ozette Road, open all year, 15 campsites, $10 per night, water, restrooms, picnic tables, fire pit or grill, nature trails, boat ramp, 21-foot RV length limit, 14 day maximum stay.

- **Queets**: 21 miles east of Queets via US 101 and Queets River Road, 20 sites, $8 per night, open all year, pit toilets, picnic tables, fire pit or grill, no drinking water, 14 day maximum stay. Campground may close in winter.

- **Sol Duc**: 40 miles west of Port Angeles via US 101 and Sol Duc River Road, 82 sites, $12 per night, water, restrooms, dump station, picnic tables, fire pit or grill, nature trails, 21-foot RV length limit, 14 day maximum stay. Campground subject to closure during low visitor use periods.

- **South Beach**: three miles south of Kalaloch campground along US 101, open May through November, 50 sites, $8 per night, 21-foot RV length limit, pit toilets, no drinking water, 14 day maximum stay.

- **Staircase**: 16 miles northwest of Hoodsport via WA 119, 56 sites, $10 per night, open all year, water, restrooms, picnic tables, fire pit or grill, 21-foot RV length limit, 14 day maximum stay.

West Virginia

1   Chesapeake & Ohio Canal National Historical Park, *see Maryland*
2   New River Gorge National River

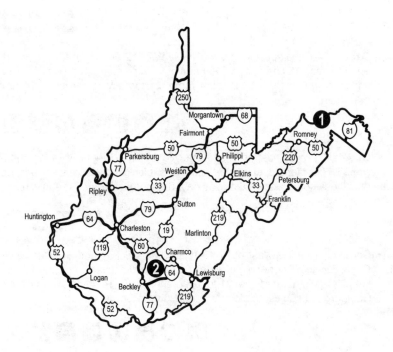

Activities Chart

Park												
2	•	•	•	•	•	•	•	•	•	•		

New River Gorge National River

PO Box 246
Glen Jean, WV 25846
Phone: 304-465-0508 or 304-574-2115
Fax: 304-465-0591

New River Gorge National River is in southern West Virginia about ten miles east of Beckley. It was established in 1978 to protect 53 miles of the New River between Hinton and Fayetteville. The park encompasses 70,762 acres of land along the New River. No entrance fee is charged.

Information is available from four visitor centers. Canyon Rim Visitor Center is north of Beckley off US 19, just north of the New River Gorge Bridge. Grandview Visitor Center is east of Beckley, six miles north of I-64 Exit 129B. It is open Memorial Day to Labor Day. Sandstone Visitor Center is in Sandstone at I-64 Exit 139. It is open year-round. Thurmond Visitor Center is in Thurmond along County Road 25. It is open between Memorial Day and Labor Day. County Road 25 is a narrow, winding road and is not recommended for RVs. All visitor centers are open between 9:00 a.m. and 5:00 p.m.

There are four primitive campgrounds in the park. Campsites are available on a first-come, first-served basis. All are located on maintained gravel roads but are usually some distance from service stations, markets, and public phones. All provide easy access to the river for fishing and swimming. Campers are required to register with a park ranger.

- **Army Camp**: about two miles west of Prince off WV 41, open all year, 11 sites, no fee, picnic tables, grills, toilet facilities, no drinking water, 14 day maximum stay.

- **Glade Creek**: located at the end of Glade Creek Road off WV 41 near Prince, open all year, five sites, no fee, picnic tables, grills, toilet facilities, no water, 14 day maximum stay. Cannot accommodate large RVs.

- **Grandview Sandbar**: located along Glade Creek Road off WV 41 near Prince, open all year, 16 sites, no fee, picnic tables, grills, toilet facilities, no water, 14 day maximum stay. Not recommended for large RVs.

- **Stone Cliff**: located off County Road 25 near Thurmond, open all year, ten sites in a sandy area, no fee, no facilities, 14 day maximum stay. Scout the campground on foot before driving in to assess water level and sand conditions, as the area is subject to flooding.

Wisconsin

1   Apostle Islands National Lakeshore
2   Saint Croix National Scenic River

Activities Chart

Park	🚐	🚴	🥾	🐎	🚶	🛶	🛥️	⛷️	🏊	✈️	🎿	⛴️
1			•		•	•	•	•	•		•	•
2			•			•	•	•			•	•

Apostle Islands National Lakeshore

Route 1 Box 4
Bayfield, WI 54814
Phone: 715-779-3398 or 715-779-3397
Fax: 715-779-3049

Apostle Islands National Lakeshore is in northern Wisconsin about 12 miles north of Washburn. The park was established in 1970 and is comprised of 21 islands and 12 miles of mainland Lake Superior shoreline. There is no entrance fee.

Information is available from three visitor centers. Bayfield Visitor Center is in the old Bayfield County Courthouse on Washington Avenue between Fourth and Fifth Streets in Bayfield. Hours vary by season but the center is open year-round. Little Sand Bay Visitor Center is 13 miles north of Bayfield on Little Sand Bay Road. It is open June through September. Stockton Island Visitor Center is open June to Labor Day and is on Stockton Island.

Only primitive camping is available. All campsites are located on islands in Lake Superior; none are accessible by road. A camping permit is required and is good for 14 days. A $15 nonrefundable fee is charged for processing a permit. The permit system allows campers to reserve campsites in advance. Private and public campgrounds are nearby that can accommodate RVers.

Individual campsites have been divided into two groups: Class A and Class B. Class A campsites hold a maximum of seven campers and three tents. They are usually within one mile of a dock and have access to well water, picnic tables, fire ring, outhouse, and bear-resistant food lockers. Class B campsites hold a maximum of five campers and two tents. They are primitive and have little access to amenities. Wilderness camping is also available, check with the park headquarters for more information.

The following is a list of islands that have designated camping areas. The class and number of sites is also listed.

Name	Class	Sites
Basswood Island	B	6
Cat Island	B	1
Devils Island	B	1
Ironwood Island	B	1
Manitou Island	B	1
Michigan Island	B	1
Oak Island	A	1
Oak Island	B	4
Otter Island	A	1
Outer Island	B	1
Rocky Island	B	1
Rocky Island	A	6
Sand Island	A	2
Sand Island	B	1
South Twin Island	A	4
Stockton Island	A	20
Stockton Island	B	1
York Island	B	3

Saint Croix National Scenic River

PO Box 708
Saint Croix Falls, WI 54024
Phone: 715-483-3284
Fax: 715-483-3288

Saint Croix National Scenic River is in northwest Wisconsin. It was established in 1968 to preserve 252 miles of the Namekagon and Saint Croix Rivers. There is no entrance fee.

Information can be obtained from the Namekagon Visitor Center in Trego near the junction of US 63 and US 53. The center is open May to October.

Only primitive camping is available. Above Nevers Dam, camping is restricted to designated sites and is limited to one night. Below Nevers Dam to Stillwater, Minnesota, camping is limited to seven days. Most campsites are only accessible by boat. All campsites are available on a first-come, first-served basis. No fees or permits are required.

Wyoming

1   Bighorn Canyon National Recreation Area, *see Montana*
2   Devils Tower National Monument
3   Grand Teton National Park
4   Yellowstone National Park

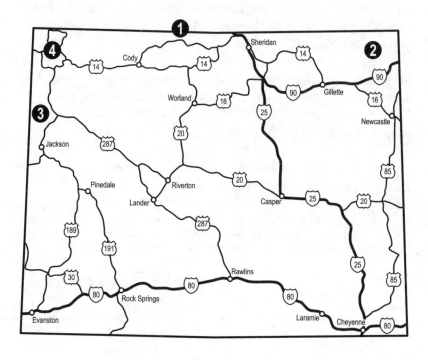

Activities Chart

Park												
2			•							•	•	
3	•	•	•	•	•	•	•	•	•	•	•	•
4	•	•	•	•	•	•	•	•	•	•	•	•

Devils Tower National Monument

PO Box 10
Devils Towers, WY 82714
Phone: 307-467-5283
Fax: 307-467-5350

Devils Tower National Monument is in northeast Wyoming about 27 miles northwest of Sundance. Established in 1906, the 1,346-acre park is the nation's first national monument. The nearly vertical Devils Tower rises 1,267 feet above the Belle Fourche River. An entrance fee of $8 per vehicle is charged and is good for seven days.

Information is available from the visitor center located at the end of the park road at the base of the Tower. It is open April through October. Hours vary by season. Features include exhibits of the natural and cultural history and book sales.

There is one campground in the monument. Campsites are available on a first-come, first-served basis.

- **Belle Fourche**: located along the park road, open April through October, 30 RV/tent sites, $12 per night, 35-foot RV length limit, picnic tables, flush toilets, drinking water, amphitheater, trails, 14 day maximum stay.

Grand Teton National Park

PO Drawer 170
Moose, WY 83012
Phone: 307-739-3300
Fax: 307-739-3438

Grand Teton National Park is in northwest Wyoming. It was established in 1929 and includes nearly 310,000 acres of rugged mountains and placid lakes. An entrance fee of $20 per vehicle is charged and is good for seven days. The park receives over four million visitors each year, primarily between Memorial Day and the end of September.

Information is available from three visitor centers. Colter Bay Visitor Center is open mid-May through September and is located adjacent to Jackson Lake about 25 miles north of Moose. Jenny Lake Visitor Center is about eight miles north of Moose along the park road. It is only open during summer. Moose Visitor Center is 12 miles north of Jackson off US 26. It remains open all year.

There are five National Park Service campgrounds. Campsites are available on a first-come, first-served basis. Backcountry camping requires a permit and is limited to designated sites. Lodging is also available at numerous lodges and resorts.

- **Colter Bay**: 25 miles north of Moose off US 89, open late May to late September, 318 RV sites and 32 tent sites, $12 per night, flush toilets, dump station, hot showers, laundry facilities, 14 day stay limit. Campground usually fills by noon.

- **Gros Ventre**: ten miles northeast of Jackson via US 26 and Gros Ventre Drive, open May to mid-October, 360 sites, $12 per night, flush toilets, dump station, 14 day stay limit. Generally fills in the evening, if at all.

- **Jenny Lake**: eight miles north of Moose on Teton Park Road, open mid-May to late September, 49 tent sites, $12 per night, flush toilets, groceries nearby, boat ramp, hiking trail, 14 day maximum stay. This is the park's most popular campground and is usually full by 8:00 a.m.

- **Lizard Creek**: at the north end of the park off US 89 about 32 miles north of Moose, open June to early September, 60 RV/tent sites, $12 per night, 30-foot RV length limit, flush toilets, 14 day maximum stay. Campground usually fills by early afternoon.

- **Signal Mountain**: 18 miles north of Moose along Teton Park Road, open early May to mid-October, 86 sites, 30-foot RV length limit, flush toilets, dump station, groceries nearby, marina nearby, 14 day maximum stay. Campground generally fills by 10:00 a.m.

Yellowstone National Park

PO Box 168
Yellowstone National Park, WY 82190
Phone: 307-344-7381
Fax: 307-344-2005

Yellowstone National Park is in northwest Wyoming, small portions are in Idaho and Montana. It was established in 1872 and was the first national park to be designated. It consists of more than two million acres of mountain scenery, meadows, and lakes. There are more geysers and hot springs here than anywhere in the world. The entrance fee is $20 per vehicle and is good for seven days.

Information is available from five visitor centers and numerous ranger stations. Albright Visitor Center is five miles south of the North Entrance in Mammoth Hot Springs and is open all year. Canyon Visitor Center is open late May through early October and is in the Canyon Village complex. Fishing Bridge Visitor Center is one mile off the Grand Loop Road on the East Entrance Road. It is open from late May through September. Grant Village Visitor Center is open late May through September and is on the shore of the West Thumb of Yellowstone Lake in Grant Village. Old Faithful Visitor Center is open late April to early November. It is on the Grand Loop Road 16 miles south of Madison Junction.

There are 12 campgrounds in Yellowstone National Park. The National Park Service operates seven of these; five are managed by Yellowstone National Park Lodges, a concessionaire of the National Park Service. Campsites in the National Park Service campgrounds are available on a first-come, first-served basis. To make reservations for sites in the five concessionaire-operated campgrounds, call 307-344-7311. Lodging is also available.

The following are National Park Service campgrounds:

- **Indian Creek**: about eight miles south of Mammoth Hot Springs Junction on Grand Loop Road, open early June to mid-September, 75 sites, $10 per night, water, vault toilets, 14 day maximum stay.

- **Lewis Lake**: ten miles south of West Thumb Junction on Lewis Lake, open June to November, 85 sites, $10 per night, vault toilets, water, boat ramp, 14 day maximum stay.

- **Mammoth**: five miles south of North Entrance, open all year, 85 sites, $12 per night, drinking water, flush toilets, amphitheater, generators permitted, limited facilities in winter, 14 day maximum stay mid-June to mid-September, 30 day maximum stay rest of year.

- **Norris**: one mile north of Norris Junction, open mid-May through September, 116 sites, $12 per night, flush toilets, drinking water, generators permitted, 14 day maximum stay mid-June to mid-September, 30 day maximum stay rest of season.

- **Pebble Creek**: seven miles south of Northeast Entrance and Silver Gate, open June through September, 32 sites, $10 per night, vault toilets, drinking water, 14 day maximum stay.

- **Slough Creek**: ten miles northeast of Tower Fall Junction, open late May through October, 29 sites, $10 per night, water, vault toilets, 14 day maximum stay mid-June to mid-September, 30 day maximum stay rest of season, 24-foot RV length limit.

- **Tower Fall**: three miles southeast of Tower Junction, open mid-May through September, 32 sites $10 per night, water, vault toilets, groceries nearby, 14 day maximum stay mid-June to mid-September, 30 day stay limit rest of season.

The following are concessionaire-operated campgrounds:

- **Bridge Bay**: 18 miles north of West Thumb Junction on Yellowstone Lake, open late May to mid-September, 430 sites, $17 per night, flush toilets, dump station, amphitheater, groceries nearby, marina and boat ramp nearby, generators permitted, 40-foot RV length limit, 14 day stay limit.

- **Canyon**: in Canyon Village off Grand Loop Road, open June to early September, 272 sites, $17 per night, flush toilets, showers, laundry facilities, dump station, amphitheater, restaurant, groceries, service station, generators permitted, 40-foot RV length limit, 14 day maximum stay.

- **Fishing Bridge RV Park**: 26 miles west of East Entrance, open mid-May through September, 344 sites with complete hookups, $31 per night, flush toilets, showers, dump station, laundry, restaurant and groceries nearby, 40-foot RV length limit, no length of stay limit. Campground is designed for hard-sided vehicles only, no tents or canvas vehicles permitted. Golden Age and Golden Access Passports not honored at this campground.

- **Grant Village**: 22 miles north of South Entrance on Yellowstone Lake, open late June through September, 425 sites, $17 per night, flush toilets, showers, laundry facilities, dump station, groceries nearby, boat ramp nearby, service station nearby, 50-foot RV length limit, generators permitted, 14 day maximum stay.

- **Madison**: 14 miles east of West Entrance near Madison Junction, open May to late October, 277 sites, $17 per night, flush toilets, dump station, 40-foot RV length limit, generators permitted, 14 day maximum stay.

Appendix A

Money Saving Programs

There are a few options frequent visitors to America's national parks have for saving money on entrance and user fees. There's the National Parks Pass, Golden Eagle Pass, Golden Age Passport, and Golden Access Passport.

National Parks Pass

This is an annual pass that provides admission to any national park that charges an entrance fee. The pass costs $50 and is valid for one year from the month of purchase. It admits the pass signee and any accompanying passengers in a private vehicle. It does not reduce the use fees charged for camping, parking, etc.

You can obtain a National Parks Pass in one of four ways:

1) at any national park that charges an entrance fee
2) online at www.nationalparks.org
3) call the toll-free number at 1-888-467-2757
4) send a check or money order payable to National Park Service for $50 plus $3.95 for shipping and handling to: National Park Foundation, PO Box 34108, Washington DC 20043

Golden Eagle Pass

For an additional $15, a Golden Eagle hologram can be purchased and affixed to a National Parks Pass (see above). It covers entrance fees charged at National Park Service areas, U.S. Fish and Wildlife areas, U.S. Forest Service areas, and Bureau of Land Management areas. The Golden Eagle Pass admits the pass signee and any accompanying passengers in a private vehicle. It does not reduce the use fees charged for camping, parking, etc.

Golden Age Passport

This passport is for citizens or permanent residents of the United States who are age 62 or older. It is a lifetime entrance pass to national parks, monuments, historic sites, recreation areas, and national wildlife refuges that charge an entrance fee. The Golden Age Passport admits the pass signee and any accompanying passengers in a private vehicle.

The Golden Age Passport also provides a 50 percent discount on federal use fees charged for facilities and services such as camping, swimming, parking, boat launching, and tours. In some cases where use fees are charged, only the pass signee will be given the 50 percent price reduction. It does not cover or reduce special recreation permit fees or fees charged by concessionaires.

A Golden Age Passport must be obtained in person at a federal area where an entrance fee is charged. There is a one-time $10 processing charge. Proof of age must be shown, such as a driver's license, birth certificate, or similar document.

Golden Access Passport
This passport is for citizens or permanent residents of the United States who are blind or permanently disabled. It is a lifetime entrance pass to national parks, monuments, historic sites, recreation areas, and national wildlife refuges that charge an entrance fee. The passport admits the pass signee and any accompanying passengers in a private vehicle.

The Golden Access Passport also provides a 50 percent discount on federal use fees charged for facilities and services such as camping, swimming, parking, boat launching, and tours. In some cases where use fees are charged, only the pass signee will be given the 50 percent price reduction. It does not cover or reduce special recreation permit fees or fees charged by concessionaires.

A Golden Access Passport must be obtained in person at a federal area where an entrance fee is charged. There is no charge for this passport. You must show proof of medically determined permanent disability or eligibility for receiving benefits under federal law.

Appendix B

The following is a list of lodges available in National Park Service areas. These unique accommodations range from luxurious inns to rustic cabins. Many require reservations well in advance. You can obtain detailed information by calling the phone numbers given or by visiting a lodge's web site.

Alaska

Glacier Bay National Park
Glacier Bay Lodge: 907-697-2225, www.glacierbaytours.com
Katmai National Park & Preserve
Brooks Lodge: 907-243-5448, www.katmailand.com
Wrangell-St. Elias National Park & Preserve
Swift Creek Cabins: 907-554-1234 May-Oct, 907-235-5579 Oct-May, www.swiftcreekalaska.com

Arizona

Canyon de Chelly National Monument
Thunderbird Lodge: 520-674-5842
Glen Canyon National Recreation Area
Bullfrog Resort: 435-684-3000
Halls Crossing: 435-684-7000
Hite Marina: 435-684-2278
Wahweap Lodge: 520-645-2433, www.visitlakepowell.com
Grand Canyon National Park
Bright Angel Lodge & Cabins: 303-297-2757,
   www.grandcanyonlodges.com
El Tovar Hotel: 303-297-2757, www.grandcanyonlodges.com
Kachina & Thunderbird Lodges: 303-297-2757,
   www.grandcanyonlodges.com
Maswik Lodge: 303-297-2757, www.grandcanyonlodges.com
Moqui Lodge: 303-297-2757, www.grandcanyonlodges.com
Yavapai Lodge: 303-297-2757, www.grandcanyonlodges.com
Grand Canyon Lodge: 520-638-2611, www.grandcanyonnorthrim.com
Phantom Ranch: 303-297-2757, www.grandcanyonlodges.com

California

Death Valley National Park
Furnace Creek Inn: 760-786-2361, www.furnacecreekresort.com
Furnace Creek Ranch: 760-786-2345, www.furnacecreekresort.com
Panamint Springs Resort: 775-482-7680, www.deathvalley.com
Stovepipe Wells Village: 760-786-2387, www.stovepipewells.com

Lassen Volcanic National Park
Drakesbad Guest Ranch: 530-529-1512 ext 120, www.drakesbad.com

Redwood National & State Parks
Redwood Hostel: 707-482-8265, www.norcalhostels.org/
redwoodnationalpark.html

Sequoia / Kings Canyon National Park
Cedar Grove Lodge: 559-565-0100, www.sequoia-kingscanyon.com
Grant Grove Cabins: 559-335-5505 ext 1603, www.sequoia-
kingscanyon.com
John Muir Lodge: 559-452-1081, www.sequoia-kingscanyon.com
Stony Creek Lodge: 559-565-3909, www.sequoia-kingscanyon.com
Wuksachi Village and Lodge: 559-253-2199, www.visitsequoia.com

Yosemite National Park
The Ahwahnee: 209-372-1407, www.yosemitepark.com
Curry Village: 209-372-8333, www.yosemitepark.com
Housekeeping Camp: 209-372-8338, www.yosemitepark.com
Yosemite Lodge: 209-372-1274, www.yosemitepark.com
Wawona Hotel: 209-375-6556, www.yosemitepark.com
Tuolumne Meadows Lodge: 209-372-8413, www.yosemitepark.com
White Wolf Lodge: 209-372-8416, www.yosemitepark.com

Colorado

Mesa Verde National Park
Far View Lodge: 970-529-4422, www.visitmesaverde.com

Florida

Everglades National Park
Flamingo Lodge, Marina, and Outpost Resort: 239-695-3101,
www.flamingolodge.com

Georgia

Cumberland Island National Seashore
Greyfield Inn: www.greyfieldinn.com

Hawaii

Hawaii Volcanoes National Park
Volcano House: 808-967-7321

Kentucky

Mammoth Cave National Park
Mammoth Cave Hotel: 270-758-2225, www.mammothcavehotel.com

Michigan

Isle Royale National Park
Rock Harbor Lodge: 906-337-4993, www.isleroyaleresort.com

Minnesota

Voyageurs National Park
Kettle Falls Hotel: 888-534-6835, www.kettlefallshotel.com

Missouri

Ozark National Scenic Riverways
Big Spring Lodge: 573-323-4332

Montana

Glacier National Park
Apgar Village Lodge: 406-888-5484, www.westglacier.com
Glacier Park Lodge: 406-892-2525, www.glacierparkinc.com
Lake McDonald Lodge: 406-892-2525, www.glacierparkinc.com
Many Glacier Hotel: 406-892-2525, www.glacierparkinc.com
Prince of Wales Hotel: 406-892-2525, www.glacierparkinc.com
Rising Sun Motor Inn: 406-892-2525, www.glacierparkinc.com
Swift Current Motor Inn: 406-892-2525, www.glacierparkinc.com
Village Inn: 406-892-2525, www.glacierparkinc.com

Nevada

Lake Mead National Recreation Area
  Cottonwood Cove Resort: 702-297-1464, www.cottonwoodcoveresort.com
  Echo Bay Resort: 702-394-4000, www.sevencrown.com
  Lake Mead Resort: 702-293-2074, www.sevencrown.com
  Lake Mohave Resort at Katherine Landing: 520-754-3245,
    www.sevencrown.com
  Temple Bar Resort: 520-767-3211, www.sevencrown.com

North Carolina

Blue Ridge Parkway
  Bluffs Lodge: 336-372-4499, www.blueridgeresort.com
  Peaks of Otter Lodge (VA): 540-586-1081, www.peaksotter.com
  The Pisgah Inn: 828-235-8228, www.pisgahinn.com
  Rocky Knob Cabins (VA): 540-593-3503, www.blueridgeresort.com

Ohio

Cuyahoga Valley National Recreation Area
  The Inn at Brandywine Falls: 330-467-1812,
    www.innatbrandywinefalls.com

Oregon

Crater Lake National Park
  Crater Lake Lodge: 541-830-8700, www.crater-lake.com
  Mazama Village Motor Inn: 541-830-8700, www.crater-lake.com
Oregon Caves National Monument
  Oregon Caves Lodge: 541-592-3400, www.oregoncavesoutfitters.com

South Dakota

Badlands National Park
  Cedar Pass Lodge: 605-433-5460, www.cedarpasslodge.com

Tennessee

Big South Fork National River & Recreation Area
  Charit Creek Lodge: 865-429-5704, www.charitcreek.com
Great Smoky Mountains National Park
  LeConte Lodge: 865-429-5704, www.leconte-lodge.com

Texas

Big Bend National Park
  Chisos Mountains Lodge: 915-477-2291, www.chisosmountainslodge.com

U.S. Virgin Islands

Virgin Islands National Park
  Cinnamon Bay Campground: 340-776-6330, www.cinnamonbay.com

Utah

Bryce Canyon National Park
  Bryce Canyon Lodge: 435-834-5361, www.brycecanyonlodge.com
Zion National Park
  Zion Lodge: 435-772-3213, www.zionlodge.com

Virginia

Shenandoah National Park
  Big Meadows Lodge: 800-778-2851, www.visitshenandoah.com
  Lewis Mountain Cabins: 800-778-2851, www.visitshenandoah.com
  Skyland Resort: 800-778-2851, www.visitshenandoah.com

Washington

Mount Rainier National Park
  National Park Inn: 360-569-2275, www.guestservices.com/rainier
  Paradise Inn: 360-569-2275, www.guestservices.com/rainier
North Cascades National Park
  North Cascades Stehekin Lodge: 509-682-4494, www.stehekin.com
  Ross Lake Resort, 206-386-4437, www.rosslakeresort.com
  Stehekin Valley Ranch: 800-536-0745, www.courtneycountry.com
Olympic National Park
  Kalaloch Lodge: 866-525-2562, www.visitkalaloch.com
  Lake Crescent Lodge: 360-928-3211, www.lakecrescentlodge.com
  Lake Quinault Lodge: 360-288-2900, www.visitlakequinault.com
  Log Cabin Resort: 360-928-3325, www.logcabinresort.net
  Sol Duc Hot Springs Resort: 360-327-3583,
      www.northolympic.com/solduc

Wyoming

Grand Teton National Park
Colter Bay Village: 307-543-3100, www.gtlc.com
Dornan's Spur Ranch Log Cabins: 307-733-2522, www.dornans.com
Flagg Ranch Resort: 800-443-2311, www.flaggranch.com
Jackson Lake Lodge: 307-543-3100, www.gtlc.com
Jenny Lake Lodge: 307-543-3100, www.gtlc.com
Signal Mountain Lodge: 307-543-2831, www.signalmtnlodge.com
Triangle X Ranch: 307-733-2183, www.trianglex.com

Yellowstone National Park
Canyon Lodge and Cabins: 307-344-7311, www.travelyellowstone.com
Grant Village: 307-344-7311, www.travelyellowstone.com
Lake Lodge Cabins: 307-344-7311, www.travelyellowstone.com
Lake Yellowstone Hotel and Cabins: 307-344-7311,
    www.travelyellowstone.com
Mammoth Hot Springs Hotel and Cabins: 307-344-7311,
    www.travelyellowstone.com
Old Faithful Inn: 307-344-7311, www.travelyellowstone.com
Old Faithful Lodge Cabins: 307-344-7311, www.travelyellowstone.com
Old Faithful Snow Lodge and Cabins: 307-344-7311,
    www.travelyellowstone.com
Roosevelt Lodge Cabins: 307-344-7311, www.travelyellowstone.com

Index

Free Newsletter for Campers and Travelers

RoadNotes is all about touring America

Subscribe to *RoadNotes* and discover unique, fun places to visit around town and off the beaten path as well as the scenic byways in between.

Learn about camping and recreational opportunities in State Parks and areas managed by the Corps of Engineers, U.S. Forest Service, National Park Service, and other government agencies that manage our public lands.

Each monthly issue of *RoadNotes* also describes gadgets and gizmos for camping and road travel, links to related web sites, and much more.

Read the current issue online or subscribe to automatically receive the free e-mail newsletter the first Saturday of every month by visiting www.RoadNotes.com.

Free Service for RVers

www.**RVdumps**.com

RVers can now easily find a public dump station at locations across the United States. Included are truck stops and travel centers, rest areas, gas stations, city and county parks, and many more. And most locations offer this service free of charge.

RVdumps.com also offers useful tips to follow when emptying holding tanks and links to other RV-related web sites. As a service to RVers, all the information at www.RVdumps.com is available for free.

Roundabout Publications • PO Box 19235 • Lenexa, KS 66285
800-455-2207 • www.TravelBooksUSA.com